he King and the Quaker

A Study of William Penn and James II

by VINCENT BURANELLI

•

.is is an astute critical study of the astonishing friendship between William Penn and mes II—"two cardinal personalities of the odern era, authoritative men who deflected political current of their time and left ting influences that still can be felt on th sides of the Atlantic." Their friendship no mere side light to seventeenth-century glish history; indeed, it is not so much friendship of a Quaker and a Catholic at intrigues us, but rather the closeness of Quaker *leader* and a Catholic *monarch*, nding together at the center of power in gland for three decisive years.

Dr. Buranelli introduces his problem thus: Nothing else in the life of William Penn s puzzled the biographers and historians much as his persistent loyalty to James II. e antithesis between Catholic monarch d Quaker subject would seem to make any al understanding between the two men probable; their presumed inability to speak one another is compounded by the cusmary interpretation of James as a would-be rant and of Penn as an apostle of religious erty; and yet Penn was not only a courtier roughout this reign but also a friend, posbly the best friend, of the King. . . . James is one of the most reviled figur͟e͟s͟ ͟o͟f͟ ͟m͟o͟d͟ n history. William Penn is one vered. How is their steadfast be explained?"

The King and the Quaker ere is a perfectly plausible ex

s so without resorting to the strategy of ring off the detractors of Penn who bee in his duplicity against the detractors talk of his stupidity, or by playing off against Penn's partisans, who violently ute either characterization.

o the arguments of Penn's critics, who t him as either fool or knave, and those his admirers, who plead "extenuating mstances," Dr. Buranelli proposes anr hypothesis to explain the Quaker's lty to James II: "Penn was loyal to es II, and he was right." His book tests hypothesis and, in doing so, makes sense hitherto baffling side of William Penn.

ABOUT THE AUTHOR

cent Buranelli was born in New York in 1919. After serving in the United es Army from 1941-45 he received a . degree from the National University of nd in 1947 and an M.A. degree from same institution the following year. In l he earned his doctorate from Camge University.

amed a Kaltenborn Fellow in Journalin 1953, Dr. Buranelli is a member of Royal Dublin Society, the Cambridge n, the Friends of the Princeton Library, the American Studies Association.

thor of *The Trial* Twayne's United has written *Edgar* ntly working on a le has contributed s as the *Cambridge Journal*, the *Journal of the History of Ideas*, the *American Quarterly*, *Ethics*, the *South Atlantic Quarterly*, and *Proceedings of the American Philosophical Society*. He is also a book reviewer for the *American Quarterly*,

THE ❧ KING & THE QUAKER

A STUDY OF WILLIAM PENN
AND JAMES II

HE KING & THE QUAKER

A STUDY OF WILLIAM PENN
AND JAMES II

BY VINCENT BURANELLI

UNIVERSITY OF PENNSYLVANIA PRESS
PHILADELPHIA

TO NAN

PREFACE ❧

There are many good reasons for writing a book, and one of the best is to fill a gap in the author's library. If you think that someone ought to produce a given volume, the most satisfactory way of getting the job done is to do it yourself. That is how the present work came into being. It is offered *faute de mieux* since no one else has attempted a realistic interpretation of the remarkable and enduring amity between William Penn and James II. The worth of the interpretation that follows may be left to the judgment of the reader, but the worth of the attempt should be self-evident.

This book deals with two cardinal personalities of the modern era, authoritative men who deflected the political current of their time and left lasting influences that still can be felt on both sides of the Atlantic. We are what we are to an appreciable degree because William Penn and James Stuart were what they were. Their friendship, therefore, cannot be relegated to a footnote on the history of England in the seventeenth century. It is interesting as a psychological study that a Quaker and a Catholic should have been so close; it is much more momentous that they were a Quaker leader and a Catholic monarch who stood together at the center of power in England for three decisive years.

Penn and James have each been the subject of many histories and biographies. The time has long since come to take a good look at their mutual relationship.

7

There is one particular facet of the Penn-James liaison that touches Americans uniquely. We are going to hear more insistently the query about the wisdom of electing a Catholic President of the United States. Anyone who wonders about this ought to read what William Penn has to say about the wisdom of allowing a Catholic to sit on the throne of England. The negative arguments of his era were very similar to those so familiar in twentieth century America : the conscience of a Catholic head-of-government is in the Pope's pocket, the claim to infallibility is inconsistent with religious or political liberty, Catholic governments are in fact never tolerant when they have the power to be intolerant, etc. Penn heard all of these arguments, and his reasons for rejecting them are not irrelevant to the practice of American democracy. (See part III, ch. IV, below.)

Some of the material in this book has appeared in the *Proceedings* of the American Philosophical Society. The author wishes to thank the Society for permission to use this material.

VINCENT BURANELLI

Penn's Neck
Princeton
New Jersey

CONTENTS ❧

THE PROBLEM

Nothing else in the life of William Penn has puzzled the biographers and historians so much as his persistent loyalty to James II. The antithesis between Catholic monarch and Quaker subject would seem to make any real understanding between the two men improbable; their presumed inability to speak to one another is compounded by the customary interpretation of James as a would-be tyrant and of Penn as an apostle of political liberty; and yet Penn was not only a courtier throughout this reign but also a friend, possibly the best friend, of the King. He refused to take part in the opposition to James II, begged his fellow countrymen to keep their heads and control their nerves when the Glorious Revolution of 1688 was in the making, and frankly lamented the fall and exile of his Stuart patron. His allegiance was so unequivocal, so openly avowed, so unapologetic, as to make him an object of interest to the government when William of Orange arrived and became William III of England.

James II is one of the most reviled figures of modern history. William Penn is one of the most revered. How is their steadfast friendship to be explained?

Admirers of Penn usually show a certain embarrassment when the question is raised, for it is not easy to condemn James without condemning his staunchest defender. It is not easy to laud Penn without lauding the sovereign to whom he owed so much. Unwilling to call Penn either stupid or deceit-

13

ful, these writers incline toward the judgment that he no doubt was a little too sanguine about the King, but that in any case he was no henchman of despotism since his purpose was to extract the patent good of religious freedom from the welter of evils in the reign. The author of the best biography of William Penn observes that "the part that Penn took in attempting to realize his noble dream of toleration, during the exceedingly difficult and inauspicious years of James II's reign, has become a cause of admiration and gratitude."

Even this biographer, however, makes no attempt to justify Penn's public support of James right up to the rebellion, much less his reiterated declarations that James was a sincere and patriotic ruler. The very eulogistic editors of selections from Penn are willing to allow that "possibly the unscrupulous and bigoted James 'used' Penn's friendship with the Stuart house to strengthen his own hand among the dissenters in an effort to gain ascendancy for Catholicism." The concession is typical.

Writers of the opposite tradition have found it easier to pass a verdict. Led by Macaulay, they have discerned both stupidity and deceit in Penn, caustically assailing him for adhering to the man whom they picture as the worst of the modern kings of England. For them there has never been any question about Penn's being right: that he was wrong is axiomatic, the only true problem being whether or not he was culpably wrong—whether he understood what he was doing, or was taken in. A few excerpts from different critics of different periods will show better than anything the general lines of the indictment.

The integrity of Penn had stood firm against obloquy and persecution. But now, attacked by royal smiles, by female blandishments, by the insinuating eloquence and delicate flattery of veteran diplomatists and courtiers, his resolution began to give way. Titles and phrases against which he

*had often borne his testimony dropped occasionally from
his lips and his pen. It would be well if he had been guilty
of nothing worse than such compliances with the fashions
of the world. (Macaulay, 1848)*

*Penn actually had the face to say that James would not
establish popery and despotism because he had promised
not to do so. (Fisher, 1900)*

*It appeared to many of his contemporaries as amazing as
it does to us, that Penn had so much apparent power over
James at this time. The King, we now see plainly enough,
was merely using Penn as a stalking-horse, as he was using
other Dissenters, such as Stephen Lobb the Independent :
the only toleration he really cared about was toleration for
Papists. Penn was gulled . . . (Dobrée, 1932)*

*No doubt the intentions of Penn, as far as they were clear
intentions, were perfectly honourable. But he was blunder-
ing: he was being misled by an infantile sense of importance.
(Vulliamy, 1934)*

*An ardent believer in toleration, Penn, who had many
interviews with James after his accession, was optimistic
or dense enough to believe that his sovereign was at heart
clement and tolerant. Such credulity is often found among
men who otherwise are unusually astute . . . (Ogg, 1955)*

*It would be easy enough to play off Penn's detractors who
believe in his duplicity against the detractors who prefer to
talk of his dimwittedness. It would be just as easy to play off
both against his partisans who demur at both characteriz-
ations. But polemical dialectic of this kind will not solve the
problem (although it proves how subjective are the opinions
about Penn).*

*Let us formulate the problem in these terms. Penn's enemies
argue: "Penn was loyal to James II, which makes him either
a fool or a knave." Penn's admirers argue: "Penn was loyal
to James II, but there were extenuating circumstances." The
differing interpretations make it possible for the King's biog-*

*rapher to refer to James' "extraordinary, indeed inexplicable,
friendship with William Penn." Yet all this implicitly sets
aside a third alternative that, if true, would make the friendship less extraordinary and by no means inexplicable. The
third alternative is to argue: "Penn was loyal to James II, and
he was right."*

*The proposition is not self-evidently absurd. It ought to be
considered seriously for at least one good reason, namely that
we may be sure of having boxed the compass of all possible
positions. The purpose of the following pages is to test the
third alternative, and to see how far it will carry us in making
sense of a hitherto baffling side of William Penn.*

THE BACKGROUND

A Penn at Court was, as such, nothing to be surprised about. It was already a family tradition when James II came to the throne. The Penns had served the Stuarts, and been favored by them, for at least two generations—ever since the times of Giles Penn, a trader of the early seventeenth century who took to diplomacy and represented Charles I in Morocco. Giles Penn is a rather obscure figure. It is with his son that the Penn–Stuart friendship begins to flower in the full light of day.

The son was the man we know as Admiral Sir William Penn, magnate, fighting sailor, molder of the English naval tradition, favorite at the Court of Charles II, and father of William Penn the Quaker statesman. Admiral Penn might be discussed from many different points of view. Here he is important as the connecting link between James Stuart, his patron, and William Penn, his son. Except for Admiral Penn the drama might not have taken place, and certainly would not have developed as it did. Hence the beginning has to be with him.

I

ADMIRAL SIR
WILLIAM PENN

THE FIRST William Penn known to history was, according to John Aubrey, "not equalled in his time for the knowledge of navall affayres." That knowledge, acquired at sea and later distilled into a code of precepts and regulations, helped to guide England's navy toward the domination of the oceans of the world. Admiral Penn shared materially in expanding the sea power that has been so preponderant an element in the world for over two centuries.

When Charles II returned in 1660, this Penn had behind him twenty years of service with the fleet. During the rebellion that overthrew and executed Charles I, he rose from captain of a ship to commander of a task force, serving first Parliament and then Cromwell. He may have been a Royalist all the time, and the alacrity with which he accepted the Restoration suggests that he was. Later he had to face the charge of being a turncoat, but to his son, at least, his "constancy" seemed remarkable because he had uniformly fought against England's foes regardless of who held power at home.

A General-at-Sea during the First Dutch War, he crossed swords, and successfully, with those redoubtable Netherlandish admirals, De Ruyter and Van Tromp. He was Cromwell's naval commander at the attempt to split the Spanish Empire in the West Indies by capturing Hispaniola. Instead of taking the island, the English were beaten back to their ships, whereupon, in order not to go away empty-handed, they invaded and captured Jamaica, after which Admiral Penn and his military comrade-in-arms, General Robert Venables, turned around and sailed for home.

They had hardly set foot in England before they were hurried to the Tower of London, a sufficiently plain warning that they would pay with their heads should they be found guilty of treason. Clarendon asserts that Admiral Penn and General Venables were in touch with the Royalists on the Continent before sailing for the West Indies and that Cromwell "could never be persuaded to trust either of them again." The Admiral was dogged ever after by the rumor that he deliberately connived at the failure of Hispaniola in order to discredit the Lord Protector. His conduct at Jamaica should have been enc ugh of a retort. His son had quite another explanation for the Hispaniola fiasco: ". . . 'twas not so much the Miscarriage of the People there, as the just Vengeance of the Almighty, for making that unjust war with Spain, and disguising the Design to the Spanish Ambassador, with reiterated Dissumulations and horrible Impostures." Presumably the "just Vengeance of the Almighty" stopped short of Jamaica.

Admiral Penn survived Cromwell's wrath. Prudently he retired to his Irish estates for the best part of the next four years, during which time he turned irrevocably Royalist, and emerged only on the death of the usurper. In 1658 he stood for Parliament, was elected, brought his family to London, and joined the circle of English leaders who had decided that the monarchy must be reestablished.

The cry for the return of Charles II became insistent. The voice of Admiral Penn may not have been among the loudest, but he sat in the Parliament that voted to bring the nation's rightful monarch to the throne and cast his vote in the affirmative. His Royalism was no sudden novelty with him. He stood so well with his fellow members, he was in such close

contact with the temper of the House, that he seems to have
been commissioned to carry its homage to the King. He was
granted a hundred pounds "for a special service," and, holding no naval command, accompanied the flotilla that crossed
over to Holland to escort Charles Stuart back to England in
triumph.

King Charles was not ungrateful for the way this subject
had stood by him when the situation was still touch and go.
Before the flotilla made landfall on the other side of the
Channel, Admiral Penn had stepped up a notch in the social
hierarchy. Knighted by the King, he was now Sir William
Penn.

Admiral Penn and Charles II

With the brilliant whirl of the Restoration, with royalty
back, and color, gaiety, music, theaters, pensions and gracious
living revived — with all this, England could relax and try to
forget the bleak tyranny of Puritan rule. It was a merry
time for men able, pliant, and lucky enough to find a suitable niche in the new order, men like Samuel Pepys at the
Admiralty, whose satisfaction with Restoration life he per-
petuated in the pages of his diary. It was a merry time for
his colleague and superior, Admiral Sir William Penn, who
became a Commissioner of the Navy in 1660.

Undeniably, Sir William had done well for himself. A
landed squire, he was forward enough in the service of the
King to become his creditor, and so well off as to make unnecessary anything so crude as dunning His Majesty. There
was a good possibility of an hereditary title for the Admiral —
an earldom, perhaps. Knight, Commissioner, Member of
Parliament, standing high in the favor of Charles II, with
even greater honors to look forward to, he had become a man
of status and stature. And he was only thirty-nine!

A bluff seadog was Admiral Sir William Penn, newly risen to prosperity on dry land, reveling in the good things of Restoration life. He was one who could enjoy a gay evening in the society of aristocrats, favorites, party leaders, and glittering military men, a fit companion for Samuel Pepys, as numerous entries in the famous diary indicate.

8 September 1660. At night sent for by Sir W. Pen, with whom I sat late drinking a glass of wine, and I find him to be a very sociable man, and an able man, and very cunning.

22 December 1660. At noon I went to the Sun tavern to a dinner, where was my Lord Inchiquin, Sir W. Pen, Captn. Cuttance, and other good company, where we had a very fine dinner, good musique, and a great deal of wine. We staid here very late. At last Sir W. Pen and I home together, he so overcome with wine that he could hardly go ; I was forced to lead him through the streets and he was in a very merry and kind mood.

Frolicsome with his equals, Admiral Penn showed the harder side of his character to his inferiors. The quarterdecks of seventeenth century warships were no school of refined manners, and he had been treading them for two decades. His reputation in the Navy was that of a strict martinet, and something more. His mind apparently never rose above the common mentality of a brutal era when to treat sailors harshly was the accepted thing. Beyond that, he had an uncontrollable temper; although not cruel by calculation, he was capable of savage outbursts when aroused. On one occasion he behaved so badly as to leave Pepys disgusted.

18 April 1661. Raining hard, homeward bound, and in our way met with two stout fellows upon one horse, which I did, without much ado, give the way to, but Sir W. Pen would not, but struck them, and they him, and so passed away, but they, giving him some high words, he went back again, and struck them off their horse, in a simple fury, and without much honour, in my mind.

Not a man to cross recklessly, Admiral Penn. He wanted others to bear that in mind when dealing with him. Advising his son about the management of the family estate in Ireland, he wrote that "you well know I yield to no man." At the same time he was a decent, conscientious, hard-working individual. His rougher behavior was hardly ever seen on land, and his son speaks of him almost always with the utmost admiration and repect.

Admiral Penn and the Duke of York

His good fortune the Admiral owed not so much to King Charles as to the King's brother and heir, James, Duke of York—he who would inherit the throne with the title of James II.

The Duke became Lord High Admiral of the Navy at the Restoration. Since he did not accept the post as a sinecure, since he requested it because he was interested in the Navy and wanted to see England's ships in fighting trim, he immediately set about examining the available personnel for assistants with seniority, experience, and knowledge. The first man to come to his attention was that renowned seaman with a pro-Stuart background and a fighting reputation, Admiral William Penn. Thus began the professional bond between them, a bond annealed and tempered by their working together, for Sir William's ability proved equal to his reputation. An associate from the start, he soon became a close friend of James Stuart. According to a later Penn :

" The duke," says Clarendon, " took Sir William Penn into his own ship, and made him captain of it ; which was a great trust, and a very honourable command ; and exempted him from receiving any order but from the duke."

This was very true but Clarendon did not choose to state
what it was more than this ; that it placed all the commanders in a necessity of obeying such orders as the duke,
wholly unexperienced in naval operations, might, by Penn's
counsel, think fit to issue to the fleet.

Serving as the Lord High Admiral's Great Captain Commander, Sir William Penn had a guiding hand in the English
victory over the Dutch at the Battle of Lowestoft (1665).
Some experts attribute to him the original plan used here of
having the ships fight in a line, and it is certain that he was
largely responsible for the code of naval instructions issued
to the fleet by the Duke of York.

The basis of the friendship between this Penn and this
Stuart is not hidden. Pepys confided to his diary the truth that
aggravated him almost beyond endurance. "*10 October,
1664.* Sir W. Pen do grow every day more and more regarded
by the Duke, because of his service heretofore in the Dutch
war. . ."

Here is not the place for a detailed examination of the
years during which the two men labored together in behalf
of English supremacy on salt water. Here *is* the place to point
out that the intimacy of the Duke of York and Sir William
Penn led directly to the subsequent intimacy of James II and
William Penn. James, becoming King, not unnaturally welcomed to his Court the son of his old friend and colleague at
the Admiralty.

2

THE PENNS
FATHER AND SON

WHAT ABOUT the son of Admiral Penn? He seemed, in the
Restoration year of 1660, everything his father could have
hoped for. Now sixteen, he was developing into that most
useful of assets to any family of the gentry, an eldest son
who might step into his father's shoes without impairing the
property, position, or prestige of the clan. Nature had made
him personable, quick of mind, robust of body. Nurture, the
solicitous care of his parents, had done the rest.

Great Expectations

William Penn's formal education began with his entrance
as a young child into Chigwell Grammar School near his
home at Wanstead, Essex. Admiral Penn singled out the
institution with sober deliberation, and his choice holds more
than passing interest. The Cromwellian rebellion was on; the
Puritan tide was rising; Charles I had already lost and would
soon be put to death. Admiral Penn held his naval command
now on the side of the rebels. Yet he selected for his son a
school that definitely was not of the newer persuasion. Chigwell, soundly Anglican, called itself "neither Papist nor Puritan." That was just how William Penn's father must have
described himself had he done so in a moment of candor.
Whether or not he thus early looked forward to a return to
the monarchy and a resurgence of the Church of England,

he fastened on a school that would give his son a kind of training precisely tailored to the Restoration climate of a decade or so later.

William Penn assimilated his primary education without any trouble. He became a proficient writer of Latin verses. He learned to express himself articulately in his own language. His lessons in deportment worked on malleable material : the mature Penn, Penn the courtier, with his aplomb and gentility showing through his stiff Quaker exterior, bore the impress of Chigwell. He obviously obeyed the rule about attending chapel services; at his age he could hardly have had any reason to rebel even if he had understood the meaning of so doing. Aubrey calls him "extremely tender under rebuke."

When he was twelve he had to leave school. Admiral Penn, fallen from Cromwell's grace, just out of the Tower, took the family to Ireland. The rest of the child's formal education came from private tutors, his informal education from the circumstance of having a celebrated sea captain and powerful magnate for a father. Through the Penn household passed some of the most important men in Ireland outside of Cromwell's adherents. Growing into his teens, young William Penn would have become accustomed to discussions about Church and State by men who hoped and planned for the day when they might influence both. He lived in an atmosphere tense with excitement and expectancy, and did not go unmoved by it.

The great day came. King Charles II was back in his palace. The men who had striven for him were now the men of authority and influence, among them Admiral Penn. The Admiral was still a comparatively young man, with years of service and the good life ahead of him. To crown his remarkable fortune, he had for a son a perfect example of what any father in his place would have wished for; so there was no need to fear even the distant future while savoring the delights of the present.

It was time to make William Penn's existence known in the proper quarters. To this end his father brought him forward at every opportunity, introducing him to the powerful and notable men of the realm, making sure that the King should become aware of his presence and identity. One day, in the not-too-distant future, there would be a place at Court for the son of Sir William Penn.

Meanwhile, the preparatory stage was not over. The scion of a distinguished family had to have the polish of the university before he could be considered ready for the fashionable world. And so on October 26, 1660, William Penn, gentleman commoner, entered Christ Church College, Oxford, as an undergraduate.

The First Quarrel

Admiral Penn had selected carefully, and he thought wisely and well, when he decided on a university and a college for his son. He wanted a place both Royalist and Anglican, a place for the training of scholars, gentlemen, and members of the aristocracy. Such a place beyond all others was Oxford University; and no Oxford college bore the necessary attributes more clearly than Christ Church.

On several occasions the College had the honor of playing host to the King and Queen. The names of noble, eminent, and wealthy families of the kingdom crowded its entry books. If the Restoration was gay, so in their own way were Oxford and Christ Church. The humorless Puritans were gone. Once again it was possible for men of good sense in religion and moderation in politics to break out their port and drink to the health of His Majesty.

To Admiral Penn the institution and the student must have

seemed perfect complementaries when he sent his son up to
Oxford. Christ Church College was a center of learning;
William Penn was already a good scholar. It drew on some
of the best families for its undergraduates; he came from a
very good family, his father knighted. It was Anglican; he
had been raised in a household and educated in a school
where no one ever slighted the claims of the Church of England. Christ Church, thought the Admiral, would solidify the
best characteristics latent in young Penn, turn him into a
poised member of the ruling class, and return him to his home
ready to enter the Court circle with the brightest prospects
before him.

It speaks well for William Penn's moral integrity, although
not for any precocious sagacity, that before his eighteenth
birthday he appeared to have ruined his future. He never
accepted the university. In later years he liked to talk about
the "Gross Ignorance" of Oxford. He recoiled from its
"hellish Darkness and Debauchery." This means in substance
that he could not abide the prevailing religion. He was as
Royalist as his father could wish; he was a scholar and a
gentleman; but he was not an Anglican. There is no telling
exactly how he became a convinced Dissenter, but the influence of John Owen must have been decisive — John Owen,
the Puritan divine and former Dean of Christ Church, who
had been Cromwell's man in the college, and who now held
forth privately as a theological mentor to Oxford undergraduates dissatisfied with the Church of England. William
Penn discovered and joined Owen's circle.

The question of Quakerism did not come up. Owen, far
from being interested in the doctrine of George Fox, regarded
its free will and anti-predestinarian tenets with abhorrence.
He himself remained a Puritan and an Independent, and
as such he proselytized among the students. The importance
of John Owen in the story of William Penn is that he

definitely carried him out of the Church of England, made a
Nonconformist of him, and strengthened in him the taste
for radical religious notions that subsequently shifted from
Puritanism to Quakerism.

For frequenting the Owen coterie young Penn was first
admonished by the authorities of his college, and then, since
he persisted, fined. Naturally a report was forwarded to his
father, in whose mind there now arose a terrible suspicion
that there was something very wrong with his son.

The news was the more shattering in that Admiral Penn
had not let the university interfere with William's insinuation
into the best London society. He brought him down from
Oxford to be present when Charles II rode past in a pre-
coronation procession, and the two Penns were in a group
recognized and saluted by both the King and the Duke of
York—a very noticeable honor for any subject. Pepys' diary
presents the Penns together many times, nor is the logic of
the situation difficult to understand. The admiral's behavior
is just what might be expected of a hopeful and ambitious
father anxious for the advancement of his son.

The Christ Church report stirred him. Something, he told
himself, must be done, and quickly. His first notion he revealed to Pepys, an old Cambridge man. "*25 January 1662.
Walking in the garden to give the gardener directions what
to do this year. . . Sir W. Pen came to me, and did break a
business to me about removing his son from Oxford to Cambridge. I proposed Magdalene, but cannot name a tutor at
present; but I shall think and write about it.*"

Cambridge was not, in fact, quite the unsullied home of
Anglicanism that Admiral Penn imagined, but even if it had
been the proposed transfer could not have been carried out.
The situation at Oxford deteriorated too rapidly for that. The
Admiral hardly had time to sort out his ideas before the
wayward member of the family was back. Pepys writes:

"*16 March 1662*. Walking in the garden with Sir W. Pen. His son William is at home, not well. But all things, I fear, do not go well with them—they look disconsolately, but I know not what ails them."

What ailed them was that "his son William" had been expelled from Christ Church. Later in life Penn described himself as "persecuted" at Oxford. Admiral Penn was in no mood to listen to the allegation, for he felt more shocked than anyone by this deviation into Nonconformity. Pepys testifies to the fact. "*28 April 1662*. Sir W. Pen much troubled upon letters come last night. Showed me one of Dr. Owen's to his son, where it appears his son is much perverted in his opinion by him; which I now perceive is one thing which hath put Sir William so long off the hookes."

It was not that Admiral Penn was an irreligious man, or even latitudinarian. A practicing adherent of the Church of England, in which he lived and died, he possessed a strain of genuine piety in his character. He was even capable of being moved by Nonconformist preaching. But he was no enthusiast heedless of everything except the call of the divine, no "fanatic" as he himself would have put it. He was not prepared to let religious scruples get in the way of his ambition, not when Anglicanism seemed so easy to accept and so right for a gentleman. "Bred his sonne religiously," says Aubrey, "and, as the times grew loose, would have had his sonne of the fashion, and was therefore extreme bitter at his sonne's retirement."

For the first time the Penns met on terms of ill feeling. Even Lady Penn was annoyed by her son's conduct at the university, and by his refusal now to listen to his father. The ex-undergraduate had been too well briefed by John Owen, and, infuriatingly, continued to correspond with the Puritan theologian. More than that, he began to visit Nonconformist meetings in London instead of going to Anglican services. His

new friends were "sober and religious People," Dissenters who
were the butt of ridicule around the Court.

Recall that at this moment Admiral Penn was rising toward
the zenith of his career — a favorite at Court, honored by the
King, patronized by the Duke of York. For the first two years
of the Restoration he looked toward a glowing future with
no obstacle between him and loftiest status to which a man
of his birth could aspire. After 1662 his own career still knew
little but success for some years; but now he was bedeviled
by the strange behavior of his son, who obstinately preferred
the dour theology, deportment, and rites of the Dissenters to
the fairest of worldly achievements. The blood boiled in the
Admiral's head as he saw his plans being overturned. He
wondered agonizingly how he might explain to his royal
benefactors and tried to think in what terms he might apologize for the ungentlemanly aberration that had suddenly
manifested itself in his namesake — whom he had recently
been presenting to them so proudly.

Ultimately, in the course of one argument, Sir William
Penn lost his temper completely. He seized his cane, gave his
upstart offspring a thrashing, and ordered him to leave the
house. In his Quaker days Penn referred to this episode as
"the bitter usage I underwent when I returned to my father,
whipping, beating, and turning out of doors in 1662."

Not long after, and largely due to the intercession of his
mother, he was back home. Admiral Penn, his gust of fury
spent, relented. He had thought the problem over and had
decided that it was not beyond solution. If neither argument
nor pleading would shake William's attachment to the out-
landish talk, dress, conduct and ceremonies of the Nonconformists, possibly a practical example of the proper kind of
life for a gentleman would succeed. Let him experience a bit
of Court etiquette, and he might take to it as avidly as one
of the gentry should. Not the English Court, not that of

Charles II : the issue would be complicated with considerations a little too delicate, and the Dissenters would still be
too close for comfort. Besides, there was a much more splendid
royal establishment just across the Channel. Louis XIV was
the premier king in Europe, just as France was the premier
nation. Surely no young man would be able to resist the
pomp, the excitement, the aristocratic gallantry of the French
Court. Admiral Penn's decision was that William Penn should
go to Paris to be straightened out.

Reconciliation

We have too little information about Penn's sojourn in
Paris. He does not tell us whether he was presented to Louis
XIV, conversed with Colbert, saw Turenne, heard Bossuet
preach, or went to the plays of Molière. We do know that he
adopted some essentials of the Gallic manner. He became
fluent in French, the language of culture everywhere in
Christendom. He began to dress like a cavalier, in ruffles and
buckles and powdered wig. He learned how to carry a rapier
with a brave air, and, moreover, how to use it, as he confesses.
"I was once myself in France. . . . set upon about eleven
at night as I was walking to my lodging, by a person that
waylaid me, with his naked sword in his hand, who demanded
satisfaction of me for taking no notice of him, at a time when
he civilly saluted me with his hat; tho' the truth was, I saw
him not when he did it. I will suppose he had killed me, for
he made several passes at me, or I in my defence had killed
him, when I disarmed him."

Penn had a special reason for reporting the incident : he
uses it to show the absurdity of punctilio when it endangers
the life of a man. He had no such reason for mentioning other
incidents in which he may have been involved and which
might be revelatory about both William Penn and the France

of Louis XIV as it crossed the threshold into the Augustan Age of modern European history.

Actually, he stayed at the Paris Court for only a few months. He did not feel at home there for all his success as a courtier. He was still worried about the condition of his soul; and toward the end of 1662 he left for Saumur on the Loire, where he enrolled as a student in the Huguenot seminary of that city.

At Saumur he found an atmosphere more to his liking. The Huguenots were the Nonconformists of France, sober, serious, earnest, people who would not let themselves be enticed or forced into the Catholic Church or turned aside from their spiritual quest by the dazzling prizes of the society around them. They reinforced in Penn the sobriety and sincerity he had brought with him from England. Most of all he was influenced by one of the outstanding men of French Protestantism, Professor Moses Amyraut, in whose house he lived as a guest. Amyraut is basic in any study of Penn's religious history, for the Huguenot theologian taught a modified Calvinism that clashed with the unyielding Calvinism that Penn had learned from John Owen at Oxford. Amyraut tried to get around predestinarianism, and although he failed, by his very attempt he shook the Calvinist faith of his student. After Saumur, Penn was in a spiritual flux such that he would abandon the creed of John Calvin, root and branch, should he meet a more humane faith to which he could give unconditional assent.

William Penn, returning home after two years abroad, received a willing welcome from his father, who was delighted with the change in him. The Penns' acquaintances were suitably impressed, including Mrs. Pepys. "*26 August 1664. This day my wife tells me Mr. Pen, Sir William's son, is come back from France, and come to visit her. A most modish person, grown, she says, a fine gentleman.*"

This period saw Admiral Penn at the summit of his prosperity. When the war with the Dutch erupted, he sailed as Great Captain Commander under the Duke of York, the Lord High Admiral, and came back covered with glory. For a messenger, the Great Captain Commander selected William Penn; for it was a perfect occasion on which to engineer an audience with the King. Charles II already knew his friend's son; and in spite of the odd reports about him, here he was appearing as part of a critical operation in defense of King and Country. The messenger described his reception in a letter to the Great Captain Commander:

> At my arrival at Harwich . . . I took post for London, and was at London the next morning by almost daylight. I hastened to Whitehall, where, not finding the king up, I presented myself to my Lord of Arlington and Colonel Ashburnham. At his majesty's knocking, he was informed there was an express from the Duke ; at which, earnestly skipping out of his bed, he came only in his gown and slippers; who, when he saw me, said "oh! is't you? how is Sir William ? " He asked how you did at three several times . . . After interrogating me above half an hour, he bid me go about your business and mine too.

The ice broken between him and Charles II, William Penn did not rejoin the fleet. He was entered at Lincoln's Inn as a student; and he resumed his classes, absorbing in the next few months enough of the law to use it very shrewdly in defense of his rights later on.

His stay at Lincoln's Inn was interrupted by one of the worst scourges ever to strike a great city — the plague that swept through London in 1665. With the advent of this horror, Penn's religious vocation revived. He began to meditate more intensely about the teachings of John Owen at Oxford and Moses Amyraut at Saumur, and to weigh those teachings against what he heard from theological rebels running the gamut of opinion from apocalyptic visionaries to Socinians. Still he could not find a satisfying creed.

In 1666 his father sent him to Ireland, hoping he might make a career for himself with the Lord Lieutenant. A soldier's life lay open to him, and he entered it far enough to learn that his natural disposition was not entirely averse to it. He even proved his ability in the field when a mutiny broke out in one garrison. He accompanied the troops dispatched to put down the disorder, and his bearing in the subsequent skirmish was notable enough to catch the attention of his superiors. The Lord Lieutenant, the Duke of Ormonde, thought of giving young Penn a real command. To Admiral Penn he wrote: "Remembering that formerly you made a motion for the giving up your company of foot here to your son, and observing his forwardness on the occasion of his repressing the late mutiny among the soldiers in this garrison, I have thought fit to let you know that I am willing to place the command of that company in him, and desire you to send a resignation to that purpose."

Admiral Penn turned down the suggestion. He was not ready to surrender the command. To his son he sent some solemn paternal advice: "I wish your youthful desires mayn't outrun your discretion." Had he foreseen the result of his decision, he would not have been so offhand about refusing to relinquish the military authority under discussion.

Late in 1667 William Penn happened to be in Cork on family business, where, attending a Quaker meeting, he glimpsed the light toward which he had been groping, became convinced that this religion held the truth that had eluded him for so long, and joined George Fox's Society of Friends. He began to appear regularly. At one meeting he got caught in a scuffle with a soldier, who protested to the authorities.

So it happened that one day Admiral Sir William Penn found among the mail from Ireland a letter informing him that his son had just been arrested at a Quaker meeting in Cork.

The Misfortunes of Admiral Penn

The letter arrived at the worst possible moment, for the career of Sir William had taken a sharp dip downward. Professionally and personally he was in trouble.

The war with the Dutch had turned out badly. In 1665 he participated with no little distinction in the English victory of Lowestoft. By 1667 the war had been transformed so catastrophically that the Dutch were able to sail up the Thames and burn part of the fleet at its moorings. Admiral Penn received a major share of the blame. "The Dutchmen's being in the river," he informed his son, "hath occasioned my great toil and labor."

He retained his favor at Court, but his enemies in Parliament were hounding him. The Duke of York wanted to appoint him to another naval command; he was unable to accept for this reason, as passed on to us by Pepys: *"29 March 1668.* I do hear by several that Sir W. Pen's going to sea do dislike the parliament mightily, and that they have revived the committee of miscarriages to prevent it." " *16 April 1668.* To Westminster Hall, where I hear Sir William Pen is ordered to be impeached."

The impeachment of Admiral Penn was founded on a charge of "embezzling goods of great value from Dutch prize ships," a charge of such tenuous substance that he easily sustained his plea of innocent. The impeachment failed. But it succeeded in preventing the Admiral from going to sea. Losing his seat in the House of Commons, he was too disheartened to fight back and resigned his place at the Admiralty. Perhaps he would have struggled longer if he had been physically well. He was, on the contrary, a sick man suffering from recurrent attacks of the gout that broke both his health and his will.

The crisis for Admiral Penn was the year of 1667–1668. One disaster after another rose up to torment him : the failure of the war, the weakening of his position at the Admiralty, impeachment, the loss of his seat in Parliament and the surrender of his post as Commissioner, the physical disintegration of his health. And in the midst of all this, his son was arrested at a Quaker meeting!

It was enough to set off the temper of a man less choleric than Sir William. He ordered his son home at once. It betokens no little apprehension that William Penn disobeyed the Admiral's command for a speedy return by pausing with the Friends of Bristol long enough to screw up his nerve with Quaker doctrine. One thing that never occurred to him was that he might give way to his father's wishes. He was so far from considering submission that he brought home a companion, Josiah Coale the Quaker preacher and missionary, to give him moral support.

The Second Quarrel

Admiral Penn waited with mounting fury. He knew something of the Friends. Once he had been not unsympathetic toward Quaker preaching, but that was during the previous decade when the views of George Fox were still an interesting novelty. Since then Fox and his followers had acquired a very different reputation. Restoration England had no patience with people who fasted for days on end while awaiting inspiration, often fell into convulsions when it arrived, made a practice of going naked "for a sign," and on several occasions put forward claims so startling as to sound like the assumption of divinity by the individual.

Not all Quakers behaved like this, but even the moderates

clung to mannerisms that annoyed the unenlightened. They refused to dress like ladies and gentlemen. They deliberately rejected the little courtesies of refined society. They kept their hats on their heads no matter who might be present, not excepting the King. In their speech they used the archaic "thee" and "thou" for the second person singular instead of the "you" that the genius of the English language had formed into the accepted convention—a usage especially irritating since the singular indicated to everyone else that a superior as addressing an inferior.

For the class to which the Penn family belonged, there was no denying the plain truth that the Quakers were a vulgar lot at best, at worst a crowd of ranting, indecent fanatics. As Sir John Robinson, Lieutenant of the Tower, once remarked to William Penn: "I vow, Mr. Penn, I am sorry for you; you are an ingenious gentleman, all the world must allow you, and do allow you that, and you have a plentiful estate. Why should you render yourself unhappy by associating with such a simple people?"

The note Pepys entered into his diary when he heard the news about Sir William's son is an adequate summation of the general sentiment. "*29 December 1667.* At night comes Mrs. Turner to see us; and there among other talk she tells me that Mr. William Pen, who is lately come over from Ireland, is a Quaker again, or some very melancholy thing; that he cares for no company, nor comes into any, which is a pleasant thing after his being abroad so long. . . ."

Pepys could afford to look at the spectacle with detached sarcasm: it wasn't his son. To Admiral Penn a general distaste for Quakerism was but the background against which was etched in sharpest outlines the anguish of a father. It was as if the son of one of the Joint Chiefs of Staff should turn Communist today.

Sir William was too much of a courtier and a gentleman

to let his feelings show at first. But an explosion was inevitable
from the moment his ear picked up the notorious Quaker
verbiage.

[William's] father kept his temper while Josiah Coale was
there, but at night, observing him use " thee " or " thou ",
he was very angry. William told him it was in obedience
to God and not in any disrespect of him. Then his father
told him he might " thee " or " thou " whom he pleased
except the King, the Duke of York, and himself, but them
he should not " thee " or " thou." But he answered he
must speak in the singular number to the King, the Duke,
and himself, which made his father very angry.

The first evening's conversation ending in complete discord,
the Admiral decided to break off, sleep on it, and then launch
a frontal attack in more secluded circumstances, away from
home and the constricting, temporizing presence of Lady
Penn.

In the morning they went out in the coach together, but
William did not know where they were going. However
the coachman was ordered to drive into the park. Then
he found that his father's intent was to have private discourse with him. His father beginning with him, told him
he could not tell what he could think of himself after he
had trained him up in learning and other accomplishments
for a courtier—or for an ambassador or other minister—
that he should become a Quaker. He answered it was
in obedience to the manifestation of God in his own conscience, but a cross to his own nature.

Before they had ridden very far through the park Admiral
Penn had passed the borderline into sheer desperation. He
could face his enemies in Parliament and the fleet without
flinching, he could endure the gout, for with these he understood the nature of the onslaught. His son's attitude was something he could not come to grips with : it seemed to him

simply gratuitous, and therefore mystifying to the point of insanity.

For adamantine firmness William Penn was extraordinary even among the Quakers, many of whom found it impossible to resist the claims of filial piety quite so rigidly. Thomas Ellwood, no less convinced than Penn, felt constrained "to make a Difference between my Father and all other Men." He therefore removed his hat when at home and addressed the elder Ellwood as "you" for some time after he had abandoned both practices in his relations with the rest of society. The distinction worried him, but he made it nonetheless. He was not alone in this.

William Penn, a stronger personality, joined the ranks of the more thoroughly committed, the heroic souls who would not be swayed from their allegiance by anything, whether the command of a magistrate or the plea of a parent. This was the obstacle into which Admiral Penn ran full tilt. "And here," relates the contemporary biographer,

And here my Pen is diffident of her Abilities to describe that most pathetick and moving Contest which was betwixt his Father and him. His father acted by Natural Love, principally aiming at his son's Temporal Honour ; He, guided by a Divine Impulse, having chiefly in View his own Eternal Welfare. His Father grieved to see the well-accomplished Son of his Hopes, now ripe for Worldly Promotion, voluntarily turn his Back on it; He, no less afflicted, to think that a Compliance with his Earthly Father's pleasure was inconsistent with an Obedience to his Heavenly One. His Father pressing his Conformity to the Customs and Fashions of the Times ; He modestly craving Leave to refrain from what would hurt his Conscience. His Father earnestly entreating him, and almost on his Knees beseeching him to yield to his Desires ; He, of a loving and tender Disposition, in an extreme Agony of Spirit to behold his Father's Concern and Trouble. His

Father, threatening to disinherit him ; He humbly submitting to his Father's Will therein. His Father turning
his Back on him in Anger ; He lifting up his Heart to God
for strength to support him in that Time of Trial.

When they returned home nothing had changed, except
that Admiral Penn now realized how little hope he might
entertain that William would ever be cajoled or shamed out
of his Quakerism. Nor did the latter become the least bit more
discreet about his connection with the Friends; instead he
openly joined them as a preacher and missionary, touring
through England and speaking to crowds everywhere. Inevitably he again became involved in the turbulence that
surrounded Quaker meetings, and inevitably word got back
to the family again. This brought Admiral Penn's patience
to the end of its tether.

Returning home, his father told him he had heard what
work he had been making in the country, and after some
discourse his father bade him take his clothes and begone
from his house, for he should not be there—also that he
should dispose of his estate to them that pleased him better.
William gave his father to understand how great a cross
it was to him to disoblige his father, not in regard to his
estate but from the filial affection he bore him. But as he
was convinced of the truth, he must be faithful.

William Penn gathered his belongings, said farewell to
the family, and went out of the house. But he was soon back.
Once again his mother had interceded for him; once again
his father had relented.

Reconciliation

The Penns, father and son, managed to live in the same
house for some time, while keeping out of one another's path
as much as possible. The dilemma might have continued

indefinitely except that William's religious vocation took him away from it. He now came forward as one of the major figures of the Quaker movement. He preached to the faithful; he defended them from their enemies in public and at Court; he began to write.

Toward the end of 1668 he published a work called *The Sandy Foundation Shaken*. It was a strong assertion of certain cardinal doctrines of Quaker theology and, for all Penn's later denials, amounts logically to a denial of the Trinity. He published it, moreover, without first obtaining a license. As a result he was arrested and thrown into the Tower of London, where he lay until the summer of 1669.

That he got out then was largely due to his father's appeal to the Duke of York. James suggested that the prisoner be allowed to explain away the writing that had brought him to the Tower; and granted so much of a mercy, Penn made the most of it. He always insisted that *Innocency With Her Open Face* (1669) was no recantation of *The Sandy Foundation Shaken*, but at least he produced an interpretation of his theology that satisfied the King's Anglican chaplain.

While in the Tower, Penn had written the first edition of his most important book, *No Cross, No Crown,* the thesis of which is that the greatest of earthly goods should be considered as dross compared to those of the life to come, a not unfamiliar sentiment, but dressed out here with all the Quaker strictures on the refined licentiousness of the Restoration. The book dealt Admiral Penn a shattering blow. The final consolation for which he could hope finally lay within his grasp: the King had offered him a peerage, the title of Viscount Weymouth. Then, at the critical moment, out came *No Cross, No Crown* with its condemnation of, among other things, honorific titles. This may not have been too much for Charles II, but it was too much for the Admiral. What good was a peerage to a man whose son and heir would have nothing to

do with it? The royal offer came to nothing. Sir William
lived and died no more than a knight.

How deeply he was hurt is shown by his disconsolate
remark that *No Cross, No Crown* was a heavy cross for him
to bear. His will was finally broken. All he could do was
resign himself to a situation that had overwhelmed him. In
one of his last letters he told William Penn: "If you are
ordained to be another cross to me, God's will must be done;
and I shall arm myself the best I can against it."

He armed himself with religion. A cynic might suggest
that there was nothing else he could do, that he took one of
the most familiar turns known to psychology; but the judgment would be too simple. Doubtless his attitude would have
been different had his son come along differently. He must
have meditated at length over the disillusionment of the past
decade, which had opened with the portent of a joyful future
for the whole family and was about to end now on a melancholy note—and all because the elder son simply would not
stretch out his hand toward the good things that lay, legitimately, within reach.

It had taken so few years to hurl Admiral Penn from the
greatest good fortune to the borders of despair! In 1660 he
was a naval commander, a knight, a Member of Parliament,
a Commissioner of the Navy, a power at Court. Two years
later, the first presentiment of an evil destiny—William's expulsion from Oxford. From then on it must have seemed to
the Admiral in retrospect that he had been through little but
the stormiest seas, the lowest troughs being his own impeachment and the rebelliousness of his son. Faithful subject and
anxious parent, he had been outraged in both capacities, his
integrity impugned in Parliament, his authority denied in his
home.

A man musing thus is likely to be susceptible to the promptings of his conscience. In Admiral Penn's case one would

expect a hardening of Anglican beliefs and a more bitter estrangement from his son. What in fact happened was the reverse : if he did not abandon the Church of England, he did become more lenient toward Quakerism. The piety native to him manifested itself ever more clearly in the form of personal rather than institutional religion. The outcome was enough to astonish Aubrey (who, however, overstates the case on the basis of William Penn's evidence): "But, which is most remarkable, he that opposed his sonne's way because of the crosse that was in it to the world's latitude, did himselfe embrace this faith, recommending to his sonne the plainness and selfe deniali of it."

Interestingly, there was another member of the family who underwent no such conversion. Lady Penn, during the times of controversy, had always been a peacemaker soothing the anger of her husband, but she did not therefore feel that he was in the wrong. Her son's preposterous goings-on irritated her from start to finish. Not long before the Admiral's death John Gay visited their home, spoke with Lady Penn, and wrote to her son that "she fell upon the strange rude way that was taken up amongst such as you of not putting off the hat and what a strange thing was it to speake to a King with the hat on and that religion should be placed in such a thing." The basic annoyance of William Penn's mother can readily be guessed : "she said your father had intended to make you a greate man but you would not hearken to him."

Although Lady Penn did not come to an open dispute with her son, she never forgave him and was not averse to letting others know it. Admiral Penn was more charitable. The last animosities had been washed out of him. A rapidly failing invalid, given over to religious meditation, he wanted a full reconciliation. So did his son. The Penn family entered a period of harmony unlike anything they had known since the specter of Quakerism had raised its head among them.

The harmony would have been unbroken except for William Penn's religious duties. Still preaching in London, he was arrested under the Conventicle Act that forbade Nonconformist meetings. Found innocent by a jury, he nonetheless went to prison because he would neither take off his hat in court nor pay a fine for refusing. The sentence afflicted him less than it did Admiral Penn, who, afraid that he would die with his son away, secretly sent to pay the fine.

The Death of Admiral Penn

He had drawn up his will naming William his executor, but he suffered from an agony of doubt about what would happen after his death, for he could not be sure that the family estate would be allowed to descend to an heir who happened to be a Quaker. The Admiral, in his extremity, bethought himself of a couple of old friends who had aided him in the past and who in turn owed him much more than money. He wrote an urgent letter to King Charles and the Duke of York, commending his son to them, requesting that they see to it that he should not suffer for his religion or his dossier of conflicts with the King's magistrates. Back from the palace came a reply worthy of Stuart courtliness, a reply expressing "the most gracious and kind assurances of their regard, and their promise of continuing the same to his son, a promise which both those princes religiously observed."

With that Admiral Penn could die in peace. William Penn, at his bedside until the end, wrote down his last words, and if the form seems a little too rhetorical for a fatally stricken man, the words a little too Quakerish for one who explicitly stipulated in his will that he be buried as an Anglican, the substance seems authentic. Here is part of it: "Son William, I am weary of the world! I would not live over my days again if I could command them with a wish; for the snares of life are greater than the fears of death. This troubles me, that I have offended a gracious God. The thought of that has followed me to this day. Oh! have a care of sin! It is that which is the sting of both life and death."

Admiral Sir William Penn died on September 16, 1670. His funeral took place after solemn Anglican rites and with the military trappings due one of his rank. If his son wrote his epitaph, it was fitting for more than the customary reasons.

THE ESSENTIAL FACTS

The death of his father left William Penn on a rather unstable footing with regard to the Court. To his advantage there was the enduring amity between Admiral Penn and the Duke of York, the pledges given to the Admiral by both Charles and James, the record of actual assistance to William Penn. The negative side of the ledger was at least as long. The royal brothers were aware of his committed Quakerism with its uncouth conduct, his flirtation with a kind of Unitarianism, his rigorist moral principles, his prison record. They had listened sympathetically when his father tried to explain the reasons for his absence from Court. They knew that he had behaved in what could only have seemed to them a grossly unfilial manner, harassing to the brink of the grave a man who had been their friend as well as his father.

With Admiral Penn gone, William Penn stood starkly alone: he no longer had anyone to entreat, explain or apologize for him, anyone to alleviate whatever antagonism he may have aroused in royal circles. Surely he must have felt some embarrassment in approaching Whitehall?

As far as we can tell, it was not so. He stayed away from the palace for three years following his father's death, but only because he was otherwise occupied with personal and religious matters. When he saw that he could use the help of royalty, he went to Court openly, frankly, and without feeling

the least bit abashed. In search of what he took to be simple
justice, he did not hesitate.

His reception justified his bearing. The King and the Duke
might have censured him, or reproached him, or suggested a
hope that his future would be less bizarre than his past. They
did none of these things. They received him with consideration and as the heir of their late friend, to whom they had
given a sacred promise in his behalf.

3

WILLIAM PENN, CHARLES II
AND THE DUKE OF YORK

THE REASON for Penn's 1673 visit was the imprisonment of
George Fox, who, in Quaker fashion, refused to take the oath
of allegiance because he could not take any oath at all. Penn
had gone to Court before to plead for the Friends. In 1667
and 1668, ignoring his father's protests, he appeared at the
palace dressed in Quaker clothes and speaking the Quaker
idiom. On neither occasion did he see the King or the Duke
of York—a contingency for which Admiral Penn doubtless
felt devoutly grateful.

William Penn had better luck in 1673. James was at the
palace, received him and his Quaker companion, listened to
their plea on behalf of the founder of the Society of Friends,
and vowed his assistance on the ground that religious practices
ought to be tolerated whenever they did not cause a breach
of the peace. After that the Duke became more personal with
his visitor. "When he had done upon this affair, he was
pleased to take a very particular notice of me, both for the
relation my Father had had to his service in the Navy, and
the care he had promised him to show in my regard upon all
occasions. That he wondered I had not been with him, and
that whenever I had any business thither, he would order
that I should have access—after which he withdrew, and we
returned."

Access Penn had from then on. During the last twelve
years of the Restoration he became more and more prominent

at Court—not a courtier in the full sense of the word (he was away too often for that), but an occasional visitor who could always get to see the King, who could always rely on a good word from the King's brother. What made his position remarkable is the fact that he did not curry favor. He went his own way in both religion and politics, doing what he considered right without pausing to ask himself how it would look to the royal Stuarts.

Religion

On religious grounds alone the reaction at Whitehall was surprising. For one thing, Charles and James did not penalize Penn for his Quaker foibles. Charles II even seems to have been a trifle amused at the sturdy and unsmiling manner in which this Quaker subject held out against the "hat honor" that was universally accepted by non-Quakers as part of the deference due to kingship. The old anecdote tells us that once when Penn advanced with his hat ostentatiously clamped down on his head, the King promptly uncovered with a flourish. "Friend Charles," said William Penn, "why dost thou remove thy hat?" The King responded, " Friend Penn, in circumstances such as these it is customary for only one man to keep his hat on."

This anecdote has to be repeated since it summarizes better than anything the attitude of Charles II : it reveals his good sense and good humor at a time when another monarch, say Louis XIV, might have taken another line. James presumably felt like his brother about Penn's Quakerism at Court.

Much harder to understand is the fact that Penn was known to be hostile to the religion preferred by Charles and practiced by James. This was Catholicism.

Had not so many of his people hated the Church of Rome, Charles II would certainly have entered it as a matter of personal choice. He was too much of a politician to go that far, too bent on keeping his throne erect amid the anti-Catholic disturbances of his reign. True, in the secret Treaty of Dover (1670) he promised Louis XIV that he would become a convert; but it seems clear that he had no intention of fulfilling this promise as long as there was the faintest chance of his being forced to "go on his travels again." He had had one taste of exile and was not minded to repeat the experience. He wanted to be a Catholic, but he wanted much more to be King of England; and he did not change his religion until he lay on his deathbed.

James *was* a convert, and a strong practicing Catholic. He had taken the step at which Charles faltered. Exactly when is unknown, but it had been well before Penn's 1673 visit. Perhaps James' first wife exerted the decisive influence on him —Ann Hyde, Clarendon's daughter, who in 1670 joined the Catholic Church as the culmination of a phase of extreme piety. In any case he had been thinking of going over to Rome for several years, so that his conversion could be attributed to a number of factors that were welded together in his mind by the words and acts of Anne Hyde.

It is a commonplace of religious psychology that the convert to any faith yields to no one in his fervor. So much was true of James Stuart, one Catholic of the Restoration in whom there is nothing of Tartuffe. He believed wholeheartedly in his adopted creed. He followed out its practical implications with an earnestness that caused his anti-Catholic opponents to label him a zealot but not a hypocrite. He was called false repeatedly, but not in his Catholicism. The honesty of his conversion was what caused him to be suspected.

William Penn had published a furious attack on Catholic doctrine in 1670, his *Seasonable Caveat against Popery,* a polemic constructed from the traditional Reformers' opinions

about the Scarlet Woman of the Apocalypse and the Beast with the Ten Horns. Penn castigated "the dark Suggestions of Papal Superstition" and "the Tribe of Men that esteem all Reason carnal, and Scripture imperfect." A comparatively moderate passage took the Catholics to task for teaching nonsense : "Their Pretense of using Tradition for a necessary Supply of the Defects of the Scriptures, is a meer Juggle, since they only evade the Clearness of the one to throw their defective Doctrines under the abused Antiquity of the other."

It is not easy to understand why Charles and James did not take offense at such rough handling of the creed they cherished. Charles possibly may be set aside since he had to turn a deaf ear to much of the same from other sources, some of them closer to him than William Penn. James cannot be set aside. He was Penn's chief support at Whitehall. He knew that Penn knew about his Catholicism. He was sensitive to the jibe about superstition that he, like all English Catholics, had to endure : he confided to the Earl of Abingdon (an Anglican) that one of his reasons for disliking the anti-Catholic laws was that "they declared him an Idolator. . . ." If James really had had the soul of a zealous bigot, one would expect a furious outburst from him as a minimum reaction to *A Seasonable Caveat Against Popery*. In point of fact, there is no reason to believe that he so much as made Penn feel uncomfortable.

The mystery does not end there. During the 1670's religion became a thorny practical problem in England as it had not been during the earlier part of the Restoration. Penn played a role in this and not always on the side of the Court. His chief transgression was the amount of credence he gave to the most terrible atrocity of Charles' reign—the Popish Plot.

The effect of the web of fictions spun by Titus Oates into the Popish Plot was not a tribute to its verisimilitude, for it had none. If the object of his myth had been the Church of

England, he would have been laughed out of court. Since he attacked the Church of Rome, he had a bias in his favor before he started : he could count on the intense anti-Catholic animosity that was always latent in England when it was not overt. Ever since the Reformation the balance of power had been shifting away from the Catholics. By 1678 they were trapped and fettered by the penal laws. Their reliance was thought to be on conspiracy and foreign soldiers. As a result a big fraction of the English people regarded them with combined abhorrence and fear and were ready to be roused against them by references to Mary Tudor or the Gunpowder Plot — or the conversion of the Duke of York to Catholicism.

When Titus Oates swore to his knowledge of a Romanist plot to kill the King and put his Catholic brother on the throne, when the justice of the peace before whom he had made his deposition (Sir Edmund Berry Godfrey) was found dead by either murder or suicide, bequeathing to us what is still one of history's classical mystery stories, the orgy of anti-Catholic violence began. Soon the Catholics of England were facing a reign of terror. The toll of the judicially murdered mounted with the weeks.

Charles II knew that Oates was a pathological liar, yet even he was forbidden by the circumstances to speak out against the fury of those hunting down victims or in favor of the obviously innocent among the accused. The most tragic moment of royal silence happened in the case of Oliver Plunket, Archbishop of Armagh.

The charges against Plunket of conspiracy to bring a French army to Ireland were as foolish as they were false. The earl of Essex, who was himself to die miserably after two more years, had known well enough when he was lord-lieutenant of Ireland what sort of man Plunket was, and he told the king that the archbishop was innocent. "Then, my lord," the king answered, "be his blood on your own conscience. You might have saved him if you would. I cannot pardon him because I dare not."

All Charles II could do was wait for the national neurosis to die down, as it did eventually. How he and his brother felt about those who believed in the Popish Plot is not doubtful. One would expect them to recoil in horror from the guilty — and the gullible — of whom William Penn was one.

At the height of the madness Penn had shown an inclination to let himself be imposed on by its absurdities. In *England's Great Interest in the Choice of This New Parliament* (1679) he called on the legislators of his country to "pursue the Discovery and Punishment of the Plot : For that has been the Old Snake in the Grass, the Trojan Horse, with an Army in the Belly of it." Demanding protection "from Popery and Slavery," he told the voters to "chuse Sincere Protestants . . . in an Opposition to the Papal Interest."

It seems extraordinarily broad-minded of Charles and James that they did not make Penn pay for these words. His utterances were very mild compared to what the more credulous were saying; he never defended the mistreatment of Catholic defendants, let alone the blood-letting; and he did not pursue the theme, being soon persuaded that he had made a mistake. But even so the uninterrupted friendship of the Stuarts that he enjoyed is an interesting phenomenon.

The puzzle of this friendship, on the side of religion alone, carries a step further. In 1673 Parliament passed the Test Act, a measure aimed at driving Catholics from the public life of England by imposing on all officials an oath against the tenets of the Church of Rome. The Duke of York could not take such an oath and left the Admiralty rather than do so. From then on he had to face venomous denunciations by his enemies, who not only forced him into exile for awhile but made a powerful bid to deprive him of his regal inheritance by introducing the Exclusion Bill into the legislature. They hoped to neutralize him politically so that he would never come to the throne. The men who insulted him worst were those, led by the Earl of Shaftesbury, who placed their reliance on the King's bastard son, the Duke of Monmouth. The Exclusion Bill came so close to succeeding that Charles, having no other means of stopping it, prorogued Parliament.

The point about William Penn is that, while he opposed the Test Act, he did not condemn it entirely but proposed substituting for it a formal declaration that would have contained the anti-Catholic clause. He was against the oath in the Test Act since Quakers could not take an oath of any kind. His *One Project for the Good of England* (1679) proposed the following affirmation : "I do not believe that the Pope is Christ's Vicar, or Peter's Lawful Successor, or that He or the See of Rome, severally or joyntly, are the Rule of Faith or Judge of Controversy, or that they can absolve Sins."

This affirmation would have thrust James Stuart from the Admiralty as surely as did the Test Act. Here if ever the James of Whig history, Macaulay's vindictive tyrant, should have swung into action. Indeed, a man with an ordinary amount of passion and resentment might have been expected to make some move against a client to whom he had been a generous benefactor and whom he had made welcome at the royal palace. What James did was—nothing. Penn not only kept up his periodical appearances at Whitehall, but James' patronage increased instead of diminishing.

This means that there must have been more pleasing aspects to William Penn, and of course there were. Most of all, he was quite free of any neurosis about Catholicism, something that must have been perfectly clear to Charles and James when they conversed privately with him. If he boldly opposed them when he thought it necessary, by the same token he could be trusted when he said things they wanted to hear. His attitude must be put in its historical setting, and then it

appears very moderate. *We* think he sounds anti-Catholic
when he shows faith in the Popish Plot or asks for an affirmation that would push Catholics from positions of trust. But in
the 1670's he sounded so reserved about Catholicism that he
was beginning to be called a crypto-Catholic and even a
Jesuit.

It may have been true, and if so James would have been
persuaded of its truth, that when Penn stood by a modified
version of the Test Act, he was only struggling for the least
harmful legislation that could be hoped of Parliament.

Before this question arose he had defended toleration of
opinion for everybody in *The Great Case of Liberty of
Conscience* (1670). If he sometimes expressed fear of the
English Catholics, it was only in a few places that are inconsistent with his considered opinion and mainly dictated by
the hubbub surrounding the Popish Plot. Prudentially he
regarded their number as too small to constitute a threat, even
accepting the worst that was said about them. Historically he
denied the worst — the charge of their loving tyranny — by
pointing to Magna Carta. Even after the passage of the Test
Act he argued : "We may see here that in the obscurest Time
of Popery they were not left without a Sense of Justice; and
the Papists, whom many think no Friends to Liberty and
Property, under dreadful Penalties injoyn an inviolable
Observance of this great Charter by which they are confirmed."

The argument was enough to infuriate the anti-Catholics
who had made the Test Act and were pressing forward with
their Exclusion Bill. For the same reason, the argument would
have been very welcome at Whitehall, all the more in that
it did not come from a Catholic.

Penn also made himself an advocate of the Catholics on
moral grounds. He thought that they had as much right as
any one to practice their religion without penalties. This put

him squarely on the side of Charles II, who in 1672 issued a Declaration of Indulgence that would have taken the penal laws off all the creeds. Parliament forced the recall of the royal dispensation and then passed the Test Act. There was one man in England who would not hesitate to face the Parliamentarians and tell them they were wrong. The Popish Plot was gathering momentum when William Penn testified thus before a committee of the legislature :

I would not be mistaken : I am far from thinking it fit that Papists should be whipt for their Consciences because I exclaim against the Injustice of whipping Quakers for Papists. No, for though the Hand pretended to be lifted up against them hath (I know not by what Discretion) lit heavy upon us, and we complain, yet we do not mean that any should take a fresh Aim at them, or that they must come in our Room ; for we must give the Liberty we ask, and cannot be false to our Principles, though it were to relieve ourselves.

Charles II felt grateful for a Nonconformist leader willing to speak that forthrightly in behalf of the Catholics of England. After all, the real problem of the moment was not so much to win toleration for the persecuted as to prevent bloodshed. Whether Charles, the politician of the Stuart family, talked James into realizing that the good in Penn's writings outweighed whatever mischief they might be doing, is beyond discovery but not beyond plausibility. What is certain is that Penn never lost his place with either; rather did he enhance it from the one reign to the next.

Distaste for the Catholic creed, temporary wobbling on the best way to deal with the Catholics of England, undeviating belief in, and support for, the right of Catholics to worship as they saw fit—that was the pattern of Penn's thought. He laid down the terms on which his royal friends, first Charles and then James, accepted him.

Politics

If Penn's attitude toward religion appeared slightly suspect, so did his politics. He never ran for office, nor as a
Quaker could he have. He did write much about the political
affairs of the day, and he entered the Parliamentary elections
by campaigning actively for one candidate of his choice.
From the point of view of the Court, he was not invariably
sound.

The opponents of Charles II accused the King of governing too much in secret, as when he signed the Treaty of
Dover without the knowledge of most of the advisors around
him. The opposition was determined to bring domestic and
foreign policies out in the open so that Parliament could
circumvent Whitehall when it chose. Penn never went that
far; but he demanded government under law, protection for
legislative and judicial rights, and the eradication of the
evil counselors who stood at the King's right hand. "By no
Means," he adjured the voters, "by no Means chuse a Man
that is an Officer at Court, or whose Employment is *Durante
bene placito,* that is, *At Will and Pleasure;* nor is this any
Reflection upon the King, who being One Part of the Government, should leave the other Free, and without the least Awe
or Influence, to bar or hinder its Proceedings."

That was a daring thing to say in view of the troubles
Charles II was having with Parliament, especially its refusal
to vote him money enough to carry on the government (which
refusal compelled him to go to Louis XIV for subsidies). It
was also a fairly venial political sin compared with the practical politics Penn was engaging in at the same time.

England's Great Interest he wrote in support of the
candidacy of Algernon Sidney, an old acquaintance of his.
Sidney would not bear examination at Court. He was a
republican. He had fought against Charles I and had opposed

the Restoration of Charles II. As if this were not sufficient to alienate the Stuarts forever, Sidney had been conspiring with Louis XIV, taking French gold with the intention of raising a republican rebellion in England: "Sidney's reputation deservedly suffers from the part which he took in the intrigues of the opposition with the French ambassador, and the fact that he received from Barillon one thousand guineas for his services."

By 1679 Sidney was back in England from his exile on the Continent, and standing for a seat in Parliament. He was, naturally, for the Country party and against the Court party (the factions that subsequently became the Whigs and the Tories). The King, naturally, did not want him in the legislature.

William Penn came out candidly, insistently, for Algernon Sidney, joining him in the campaign, describing him to the electorate as the type of man who would back their interests against anyone should they send him to Parliament. At Guildford in Surrey, Sidney seemed to have won the election, only to be disqualified on a technicality. Penn considered the proceedings grossly illegal, urged Sidney to appeal to Parliament, and sought to hearten him with a personal letter which contains the line: "Thou, as thy friends, hast a conscientious regard for England; and to be put aside by such base ways is really a suffering for righteousness."

Later that same year Sidney entered an election at Bramber in Sussex. Penn, ignoring the obvious determination of the Court party to keep his candidate out of Parliament, went into the campaign again. For a second time it was in vain; for a second time Penn held that Sidney had been cheated.

So did Sidney, who, evidently embittered by the experience, turned to the stronger methods of conspiracy and assassination. He entered the Rye House Plot. The facts surrounding this famous attempt to kill Charles II and the Duke of York are by the nature of the case very difficult to get at. Sidney's execution after its failure has often been condemned as mere revenge by the Court, but the latest authority on the Rye House Plot declares him guilty as charged : "Shaftesbury had been the directing force behind the whole of the 1682 conspiracy. After his departure the plot was maintained and coordinated by a new member of the inner circle, Algernon Sidney."

Sidney's actual guilt, the justice or injustice of his execution, is of no critical import in discussing the relation of Penn to the Stuarts. *They* thought him guilty and rightly punished. James informed William of Orange that "Algernon Sidney is to be beheaded on Friday next on Tower Hill, which, besides the doing justice on so ill a man, will give the lie to the whigs, who reported he was not to suffer."

How William Penn, given his past association with "so ill a man," could have been welcome at a Stuart Court is a problem that almost passes understanding. The astounding thing is that we do not find any change in this status. Two years after the elections in which he challenged the King so vigorously, he received Pennsylvania. During his first visit to his colony, the Rye House Plot failed and his political champion was executed. If on his return Charles or James mentioned his deceased friend in recriminatory words, the evidence has disappeared — a pretty good indication that there never was any such evidence.

As with religion, the major reason must be that there is another side to the political coin. While campaigning Penn would emphasize the rights of people and Parliament against the Crown. At other times he would express opinions just as strong about the rights of the King of England against any other forces in the realm. This distinction should be remembered when in the reign of James II he is accused of wanting to turn monarchical rule into tyranny.

During the reign of Charles II he had already thought out the broad lines of his political theory. He knew the law ever since his stay at Lincoln's Inn; he had read the masters of political thought whether at Oxford or Saumur or on his own; he was familiar with the history of Rome and England and Renaissance Italy. He tried to put his ideas into practice when electioneering and pamphleteering. He is systematically for Parliament *and* King. Even in *One Project for the Good of England* he made his modified version of the Test Act come out on the King's side while arguing against Catholicism as the more exaggerated Catholics understood it, against the right of the Pope to depose secular rulers. Part of Penn's proposed affirmation reads like this: "I, A.B., do solemnly, and in good Conscience, in the Sight of God and Men, acknowledge and declare that King Charles the second is Lawful King of this Realm, and all the Dominions thereunto belonging."

If Penn does not mention James in this clause of his declaration, and there was no reason for him to do so, yet the implications for the succession were there. The sole test for a ruler of England was that he should be the legitimate eldest son or daughter of the last ruler, or failing that, the nearest blood relation. Religion should have nothing to do with it. Therefore the Pope had no authority to depose a heretic, nor did any faction of Englishmen have the authority to bar a Catholic. Penn was more than adamantly opposed to the Exclusion Bill: he regarded it as a monstrous usurpation by a group in Parliament, an infringement of the rights of the Crown, and an insult to the one true heir to the throne.

Once again the royal brothers must have been moved by Penn's sincerity. He would come right out and announce his opposition to men or policies they backed; no less openly would he defend against people and Parliament those Court measures, and they were many, of which he approved.

Charles II could understand him in both guises and was too much of a diplomat to expect constant support from anyone but a sycophant. James, not so much of a diplomat but a personal friend as Charles was not, obviously felt that there was no reason to become angry, or at least to stay angry, with William Penn.

The Logic of the Relationship

Doubtless Charles II and the Duke of York were willing to ignore the peccadilloes of Admiral Penn's son, balanced as they were by evident and helpful virtues. Some critics have suggested that the Stuarts were "using" Penn all the while. They point to his work in defense of Charles' Declaration of Indulgence, which they describe as part of a Romanist conspiracy. For some reason these same critics never point to his advocacy of Algernon Sidney or his formula for retaining the anti-Catholic clause of the Test Act.

Of course the King gained something by having a Quaker leader to speak for him on issues like religious toleration and the rights of the Crown. Penn's voice would be heard by Dissenters who would not listen to Catholics or Anglicans. But no one had to maneuver him into speaking, for he was quite ready to do so on his own account. The King did not persuade him to promote freedom of conscience; his desire to promote it was, as much as anything, what brought him to Court in the first place and kept him there thereafter. Had Penn dropped toleration, Charles would have got rid of him. Had Charles dropped toleration, Penn would have abandoned him. It worked both ways.

In all this Penn had no official status. An arch-enemy of the Stuarts such as Shaftesbury could, by force of political circumstances, make the King accept him. With Penn the only thing on which he could rely was personal friendship, a fragile bond where royalty was concerned. That he never lost it is a tribute to his character, intelligence, and ability as well as to the magnanimity of his royal friends. They enjoyed his company, he enjoyed theirs—which could be the basic motive behind this Penn–Stuart relationship. It would explain better than anything why any antagonism that may have come between them was only momentary.

Penn's gain from the relationship is obvious. Repeatedly he went to Court to get justice and mercy for the afflicted members of his faith. Repeatedly he got both, generally in the first instance from the Duke of York, who had the authority to decide which cases were worth bringing to the attention of the King. Penn hoped that religious toleration would come to England through Charles II. The failure of the Declaration of Indulgence and its aftermath disillusioned him, at least for the moment. He held, however, another card in his hand; and in 1681 he threw it on the table. He asked the King to grant him American land beyond the Delaware in place of the claim on the Crown left by Admiral Penn.

Charles could have proven difficult to deal with. It was only two years since the Sidney incident, (and Penn had not broken with Sidney: he would consult him now about the right kind of government for Pennsylvania). It was only two years since Penn had written as if the Popish Plot were authentic. James had another reason besides these to be refractory. He held vast areas of the New World based on New York and claimed jurisdiction down the Delaware to Maryland. A group of Quakers administering West Jersey disputed his right to tax all cargoes moving on the river, won their case in court, and in the process came very close to offering him a gratuitous insult: "To exact such an interminated tax from English planters, and to continue it after so many repeated complaints, will be the greatest evidence of a design to introduce, if the Crown should ever devolve upon

the Duke, an unlimited government in old England." One of
the Quakers who thus challenged Penn's patron was Penn
himself.

Nevertheless Penn encountered no opposition when he
made his plea for Pennsylvania. Charles II, having no money
to pay what he owed the Penns, was glad enough to let this
Penn found a colony that would be a haven for Englishmen,
and Continentals too, harassed by religious intolerance. The
Duke of York, far from being an obstacle, backed Penn's
appeal and then extended his own patronage by adding to
the province thus awarded the three lower counties leading
to the mouth of the Delaware River at Delaware Bay.

The following year Penn was across the Atlantic setting
up his Pennsylvania administration. During his absence the
Rye House Plot came to light and Algernon Sidney was
executed. The men implicated being Dissenters, some of
them old Cromwellians, royal policy took a sharp turn against
the sects. The "Tory reaction" set in. Penn, returning home
in 1684,

> found things in generall with another face than I left
> them : [the King and Duke] sour and stern and resolved
> to hold the Reins of Power with a stiffer hand than here-
> tofore, especially over those that were observed to be State
> or Church Dissenters, conceiving that the Opposition which
> made the Government uneasy came from that sort of
> People, and therefore they should either bow or break.
> This made it hard for me, a profest Dissenter, to turn
> myself—for that Party having been my Acquaintance, my
> Inclination, and my Interest too : to shift them I would
> not, to serve them I saw I could not, and to keep
> fair with a displeased and resolved Government, that had
> weathered its point about them, humbled and mortified
> them and was dayly improveing all Advantages against
> them, was a difficult task to performe.

The Penn of five years before probably would have published a political tract supporting the Dissenters against the Crown and might even have made some kind of political demonstration. The Penn of 1684 had changed too much for that. A colonizer, already powerful and with the promise of wealth to come, dependent on the King's good will to maintain his position in Pennsylvania, he could not longer afford to plunge into the party maelstrom without first looking over his shoulder to see who would get splashed. As he hints, Charles and James, whose lives had been in jeopardy, were for once prepared to repay him with some asperity should he come to the defense of their opponents. Accordingly: "I cast about in Mind what way I might be helpfull to the Publick, and as little hurtfull to my concerns as I could."

His words imply a personal reorientation befitting his new status as a proprietor. From then on he would lean more strongly toward the Court in both religion and politics. Prudence dictated that he do so. Less egocentric motives did too. Possibly the revelations about Sidney disturbed him. The Rye House Plot, in any event, must have horrified him as one who hated violence, as a Royalist, as a friend and client of the intended victims. The Parliamentary turmoil about excluding the Duke of York from the throne had disgusted men less close to the throne than Penn. Shaftesbury, discredited but saved from the Tower by an anti-James jury, had fled to the Continent, where he had died an embittered exile. The proprietor of Pennsylvania, himself caught up in the problems of governing a people who had to be conciliated and would soon become recalcitrant, looked at the English situation from a new perspective.

All this allowed Penn to change his emphasis. That he did so without concessions, distinctions, or equivocations is not to be argued. What can be said to his credit is that he did not contradict himself on fundamentals. If his political behavior changed, his political theory did not. Besides, one constant, the determining and indispensable constant, endured without change. The King and the Duke still wanted universal religious freedom. Parliament still stood out in opposition to freedom for Catholics. Penn could cultivate his privilege at Court no more effectively than by reiterating at every turn the principle in which he believed beyond all others: "Upon the whole matter, I found no point so plain, so honest, so sensible, that carryed such weight, conviction, and compassion with it, and that would consequently find an easier reception and more friends, than Liberty of Conscience, my old Post and Province."

Penn tells us that he urged Charles II to continue trying for religious toleration throughout the kingdom and for everyone. He also tells us that his humanitarian efforts he concentrated on the alleviation of the suffering of individuals, and that James still reacted favorably to this kind of appeal. Thus Richard Vickris had been imprisoned for refusing to take the oath of allegiance. James promised to intercede for Vickris with the King: "And the Duke was as good as his word. He was pardoned."

The situation of 1684 did not last for long. Charles II died in 1685. The Duke of York became King of England — James II. Penn was satisfied by the change: his chief benefactor was now his sovereign. Moreover, he preferred James to Charles because, although indebted to both, he judged the latter too immoral in his private life to lead the kingdom forward into an era of honor and justice. Penn thought (and this is the point to be elucidated) that James was a better hope for a settlement based on all-round sufferance, toleration and agreement to disagree. Also, he had always been closer to James so that a permanent niche at Court was open to him, and he would not balk at stepping into it.

A fresh page had been turned in the life of James Stuart. No less was this true of William Penn.

4
THE COURT
OF JAMES II

In the year 1685 Penn and James had known one another for a quarter of a century—the span of the Restoration. They had been on a personal footing for twelve years—ever since Penn's 1673 visit to Court. They had been extremely close and intimate friends for at least four years—from the time of the Pennsylvania grant. Consequently they both assumed that, the one becoming King, the other would come to Court. Penn had not been a courtier during the reign of Charles II. With James II he was a courtier from the beginning of the reign until its collapse.

At the moment of James' accession these two men were on such terms that each ought to have been capable of real insight into the character, attributes, habits, strengths, weaknesses, and foibles of the other. They were neither recent acquaintances nor too young to possess mature judgment. James was fifty-one, Penn forty-one, and both had seen much of the vicissitudes of life. They were divided by obvious differences of personality and opinion. They were also united by strong similarities.

King and Subject: The Psychology of Their Relationship

Everything in the reign is connected with religion. Except for the Catholicism of James II, he would never have lost his throne. Except for Penn's loyalty to a Catholic, he would never have mystified his friends or infuriated his enemies.

Penn and James had this primary quality in common, that they accepted religion with the total commitment of converts. Both freely judged and then adopted the tenets of a particular faith. Both obeyed the injunction to make those tenets effective in their daily lives, uniting belief and practice despite the hostility of the world around them. In consequence the one lost a throne, the other endangered his patrimony and endured injuries from slander to imprisonment.

James craved institutional religion. He accepted the traditional scheme of a church, a hierarchy, a sacramental system. That was one reason why he did not turn against the Church of England as soon as he became a Catholic: the High Church theology looked to him like a near approximation to Catholicism. This misapprehension contributed greatly to his fall.

Penn was basically, radically, anti-institutional in his religion. He held for personal inspiration — the Inner Light of Quakerism — as the only valid guide to belief and conduct. He disliked cathedrals, bishops, and sacraments, which, seen from his theological perspective, were external hindrances in the quest for salvation. He therefore opposed the Church of England, and a fortiori the Church of Rome.

The dichotomy between institutional and personal religion can, however, be over-emphasized. Catholicism has a place for the direct enlightment of the individual; and the strangest thing about James Stuart is that in this respect he rivals, in fact exceeds, William Penn. James' last years brought him a reputation for heroic sanctity, saintliness in the technical sense — a direct and personal response to the divine afflatus that goes beyond anything attributed to Penn. If James ever evidenced a spark of "heart religion" in his earlier days, if Penn ever divined it, then the manner in which they were drawn together is the easier to understand.

Given their two attitudes, monarch and subject alike were bound to abhor Puritanism. That James did so is patent. Penn's aversion was at least as great. He had deliberately thrown off the Calvinism taught to him by John Owen at Oxford and Moses Amyraut at Saumur; and as he loved Quakerism with the warmth of a convert, he hated Calvinism with the anger of an apostate. Coming to a belief in free will and salvation for all, he would give the lie to Calvinist determinism and salvation for the elect alone. In his polemical works he anathematizes the "fearful Tale of Predestination," and scores the Calvinist Puritans in these terms: "You generally scoff at Revelation as being ceast; most of you also abetting God to have ordained a Remnant absolutely to Salvation, and consequently making Sin as well as Torment unavoidably necessary to the major Part; whereby the Glorious God of Mercy is represented more infamously unjust than the worst of Men."

James and Penn were not rendered mutually antipathetic by their respective creeds. Penn was willing to admit some good in Catholicism, as when it produced Magna Carta. James, for his part, admired the Quaker way if not the theology of the Friends. At their 1673 meeting he told Penn "that he looked upon us as a quiet industrious people, and tho' he was not of our judgment, yet he liked our good lives."

They were completely united in their hope for immediate religious toleration in England. Each had seen his co-religionists oppressed by the penal laws; and James wanted the laws removed from the Catholics, Penn from the Quakers. They were, in 1685, fully prepared to help each other in this.

After religion, politics. King and subject could scarcely be unanimous about the situation in England. They were, however, less widely separated than might be thought. They stood alike for a strong central government, James thinking specifically of kingship, Penn being the more philosophical and relating the notion to the universal experience of human society. At home both were Royalists, James for self-evident reasons, Penn because he thought monarchy the best form of government, and the English monarchy providentially instituted and guaranteed by historical usage. The latter point he made while addressing a Parliamentary committee in 1678 : "We believe Government to be God's Ordinance; and next, that this Present Government is established by the Providence of God and Law of the Land."

Penn's attitude to the English monarchy and the Stuart dynasty was motivated partially by the event that had within his own lifetime interrupted both. He abominated the memory of the Great Rebellion and the man who had led it.

James II hated Oliver Cromwell as the regicide who had murdered his father. Penn hated the Lord Protector for disgracing *his* father. But there were more objective reasons, religious and political.

Recoiling from Puritan theology, Penn recoiled from the public behavior to which it led: "The Unreasonable and Unmerciful Doctrine of absolute Election and Reprobation put in Practice." "O what," he asks, "did not the Bloodthirsty Spirit in its Day? These were the great pretending Presbyterians, Independents and Anabaptists, Fighting, Knocking, Kicking, Robbing, Imprisoning and Murthering an Innocent People."

The "Innocent People" were, needless to say, the Quakers. They suffered brutally during the Cromwellian despotism, and Penn was unwilling to let the fact be forgotten. Still, this is one time when he might have given the devils their due. The Puritans had had to deal with the Society of Friends in its early, heroic, charismatic phase, when the members still shocked conventional usages on principle, when they courted martyrdom at the hands of mobs as well as magistrates, when

George Fox was rolled in the mud by rowdy gangs because
he invaded churches and disturbed congregations. Penn
speaks of the Quakers as if they had always been the respectable moderates among whom he moved.

Of the men who made the Great Rebellion he remarks : "I
can never think (unless better informed) that any Age hath
so much as equalled them in a Treacherous Hypocrisy." For
example, "the Independents themselves, held the greatest
Republicans of all Parties, were the most Lavish and Super-
stitutious Adorers of Monarchy in Oliver Cromwell, because
of the regard he had to them; allowing him, and his son after
him, to be *Custos Utriusque Tabulae*; over all Causes, as well
Ecclesiastical as Civil, Supreme Governour." As for the Lord
Protector, he was, says Penn, "the English Phocas."

It was a strong statement. Educated Englishmen would
pick up the reference from their reading in the history of
the Byzantine Empire. A centurion with the troops in Thrace
at the turn of the sixth century, Phocas raised the standard
of revolt, marched on Constantinople, seized power, and put
the Emperor Maurice to death. He then conducted a reign of
terror in which he hunted down suspects until his insane
barbarities proved more than the Byzantines could stand.
They rose in arms, overthrew him, and put the great Heraclius
in his place. The usurper was executed, his corpse treated with
indignities and cremated.

Penn took Phocas' career of rebellion, power, crime, and
retribution to be a parallel to that of Oliver Cromwell. The
equation Cromwell : England : : Phocas : Byzantium did
nothing to harm Penn's reputation at a Stuart Court.

If the English dynasty had been legitimately restored,
could it be said that Charles II had wielded his legitimate
authority wisely? James II thought that in important respects
the answer had to be "no." Charles had been pliable when
James would have had him obdurate. Charles had felt his

way gingerly among the tangle of men and principles and
pressures that could upset the throne again. James was
resolved to be bolder. He could not forget the Popish Plot,
the abominations of which he was sure could have been cur-
tailed, perhaps halted, by a blunt lead from Whitehall. This
postulate, too, hurt his reign; for the times needed tact from
any monarch, and demanded it from a Catholic monarch.
Charles may have been too hesitant. James was certainly
too resolute.

Penn had no occasion such as James had to ruminate at
length about the relation between the authority and the
power of the Crown. He did, nonetheless, agree that Charles
II should have resisted the forces ranged against him to the
extent of persisting in the search for "a True Liberty of
Conscience." He was prepared to abet James II should he in
turn take up the search.

Any consideration of politics in a dual sketch such as this
must view the principals with reference to colonizing the
New World. As Duke of York, James had gained the province
named after him, with all its problems and all its promise.
Penn had gained Pennsylvania. Their dialogue about their
colonies, once begun, never lapsed; and it was a true dialogue,
not a one-sided monologue, since Penn possessed proprietary
power so great as to be quasi-royal.

Now King, James was more of an imperialist than ever.
Penn the proprietor followed him in this. The Quaker statesman has always suggested the pacifist more readily than the
imperialist : he was the author of one of the most famous
plans for peace through a union of the nations. He also drew
up a scheme for uniting the English dominions in America,
and this was *not* a pacifist project; for he explicitly mentions
the military strength that might be brought to bear on the
French in Canada. The most remarkable of his purposes
under this heading was to settle the frontiers of English

America along the natural boundaries provided by the continent. During Queen Anne's War (the War of the Spanish Succession in Europe) he wrote to the Duke of Marlborough to urge that these natural boundaries be written into any peace treaty.

> The English Empire on the continent lies upon the south side, and we claim to the North Sea of Hudson's Bay; but I should be glad if our north bounds might be expressed and allowed to the south side of St. Lawrence's River that feeds Canada eastward, and comes from the lakes westward, which will make a glorious country ; and from those lakes due west to the River Mississippi, and traverse that river to the extreme bounds of the continent westward ; whereby we may secure one thousand miles of that river down to the Bay of Mexico, and that the French demolish, or at least, quit all their settlements within the bounds aforesaid.

Penn was not prepared to fight the French for North America; but a war being already on, he wanted his country to take advantage of the peace negotiations to accumulate as much of the New World as possible. No more than James II (or William Pitt for that matter) did William Penn underestimate the natural fitness of the English race to run an empire.

Penn's stand on religion and politics was obviously of the first importance to his place at the Court of James II. What about the more personal axis joining the two men ?

Both wanted greater decency at the palace. They wanted a change from the atmosphere that prevailed under Charles II. James II was no Merry Monarch, nor did William Penn wish that he were. The Quaker no longer felt ill at ease in approaching his sovereign; no longer need he step fastidiously around the profligacy, ribaldry, and general loose living that so recently had been everywhere — with the King setting the example for everyone to imitate. Although anti-Calvinist in his theology, Penn was almost a Puritan in his morality. James II never reached Penn's level in his private life, but compared to his brother he might be called a Puritan without stretching the term out of recognition.

James II, sterner in his morals, was sterner in pursuing his objectives, stiffened by native temperment and by his axiom about not making the cautious mistakes of his predecessor. His rashness had come out in war in the form of bravery, in religion in the form of candid avowal; it would come out now in the form of obstinacy and an inability to compromise.

Penn was not a personage grandiose enough to gamble for such stakes as the English throne, although within the limits dictated by his station he was so much of a rigorist that he had more than once imperiled his career. The man who had been expelled from Oxford, twice dismissed from home by his father, imprisoned several times, and smiled at by courtiers because he *would* play the Quaker even with the King—such a man was in no position to condemn intransigence in anyone else. Did James ever use that rebuttal when Penn became critical of him? No one knows. But we do know that Penn became critical: experience had knocked sufficient sharp corners off his personality to permit that.

Each of these men was loyal to old friends and old principles. In exile James spoke as he had spoken while on the throne; and he welcomed to Saint Germain, for more than selfish reasons, those who had adhered to his cause. After the Revolution of 1688 Penn spoke as he had spoken while James was on the throne, and refused to pretend that he had been anything but James' very good friend.

James II has not often been called magnanimous. A multitude of books have presented him as implacably vindictive, always nursing grudges, never forgiving anyone who flouted his will. Penn could have testified to the contrary. James, as noted above, never made him pay for his anti-Court indis-

cretions like professing some faith in the Popish Plot. Penn
did not commit these indiscretions in a corner; he went ahead
publicly and flagrantly; and he continued to be patronized
by James Stuart. If it was not magnanimity in James, it was
nearer to that virtue than to vengefulness. As for Penn, he
knew how to forgive his enemies despite his occasional wasp-
ishness with them, but he was acting in Christian charity
rather than with the grand gesture of Aristotle's magnanimous
man. However the attributes just mentioned may be defined,
neither James nor Penn offended the other by an unwillingness to forgive and forget.

Neither magnanimity nor charity made either ready to
accept what they considered encroachments on their legitimate authority. James' wrath is part of his biography. Penn
was capable of petulant asperity. When his colonists in Pennsylvania went their way instead of deferring to his proprietary
rights in a manner befitting his Holy Experiment, he adjured
them : "For the love of God and me and the poor country
be not so governmentish, so noisy and open in your dissatis-
factions." His ideal was a legislature freely debating the
affairs of government, and freely endorsing the administration he was giving the colony.

The two were matched in one leading deficiency. Neither
showed the faintest signs of a sense of humor. Had James
enjoyed his brother's capacity for laughter, especially at himself, he would have been better equipped to face his opponents; he would have known how to keep his temper instead
of demeaning himself by shouting at them. Had Penn been
able to see the amusing side of life, he would have moved
along with fewer jolts and might have helped James to do
the same. In their relations with one another, in their relations with other men, they were simply too austere, too
deadly earnest, too little tempted to be lighthearted about
frustrations and disappointments.

Their conversation must have been marked by *some* virtues, although clearly not by gaiety. James was no great talker, but he was a good listener when not annoyed by an unpleasant theme. Penn did not annoy him; and we have the word of so competent an authority as Dean Swift that Penn, who loved to talk, could talk well: "He spoke very agreeably, and with much spirit."

Penn and James never lacked subjects for their conversation — the King's old friend Admiral Penn, the King's past connection with William Penn, New York and Pennsylvania, power and freedom in religion and politics, the existing dilemmas of Church and State. They discussed the penal laws that were weighing on their respective religions — the Test Act, for example, still on the books, still keeping Catholics out of office, still tripping up Quakers who could not take the oath.

They had one special experience in common. Both had suffered, and were then suffering, from a caricature of their motives. To mention a notorious instance, they were accused of liking the cruelty with which prisoners were treated. Repeating this accusation, a later historian, Macaulay, even uses a strikingly similar form of words in each case, referring to Penn as one "for whom exhibitions which humane men generally avoid seem to have had a strong attraction," and declaring that James "seemed to take pleasure in the spectacles which some of the worst men then living were unable to contemplate without pity and horror." It has often been pointed out that Macaulay's thesis is not proven just because James, accepting the contemporary penal theory, believed in the efficacy of torture; and the thesis is none the sounder just because Penn accompanied some condemned wretches to their executions. The inference is that Penn and James developed a mutual sympathy because they were being pilloried in the same way, almost in the same terms.

The few psychological notes set down here are not enough to portray either subject in the round, but that is not their function. They are merely preliminary hints about what those two friends saw in one another. They are indicative of the truth that neither was prevented by any mental block from clasping the hand of the other. That they did clasp hands is the fact to be pursued further.

Penn the Courtier

On the basis of what has been said, little mystery attaches to William Penn's attendance at the Court of James II. The confidant and client of the King had no reason for suddenly declining either his amity or his support. The proprietor of Pennsylvania was no man to shy away from authority, the political theorist no man to disdain political influence, while the protagonist of religious tolerance discovered an entirely new alignment of forces from the collision of which might result freedom of conscience if only he acted energetically enough on the highest level.

The sole difficulty that called for explanation was why any Friend should be willing to remain at Whitehall : the phrase "Quaker courtier" appeared to be a contradiction in terms.

Penn had two answers to the complaint when he heard it from members of his sect. First of all, he never gave up the essentials of Quakerism. He made certain concessions on incidentals (such as not wearing a hat at royal audiences so that the question of doffing it to the King would not come up); but Macaulay's insinuation that the Quaker tended to disappear behind the courtier is without foundation in the surviving evidence.

Secondly, Penn insisted with perfect truth that his presence at Court was one of the best defenses the Quakers had at a time when they could use all the protection they could get.

James, when Duke of York, had always been willing to help
Penn rescue individuals suffering for their religious beliefs and
practices. Since James was now on the throne, Penn could
operate the more effectively as an advocate or go-between;
and this was seen within a year of the coronation when James
II ordered over a thousand Quakers to be released from their
cells. *These* Quakers were certainly not displeased by the
work their comrade was doing at Court.

It was not the religious people who were most aggravated
by the confidence reposed in Penn by the King. As might
be expected, many a courtier envied him. The following
testimony comes from a Dutch Quaker in close touch with
the English Friends.

And the King often commanded privacy, not for one but
for several hours at a time, in which he discussed many
affairs with Penn, and meanwhile delayed receiving his
greatest nobles, who remained in the anteroom waiting
for an audience with the King. Finally one of them,
either put out by the proceeding because it made one many
equal to the rest, or else of an impatient disposition and
considering the delay a slight, protested to the King, saying
that when he closeted himself with Penn he did not pay
enough attention to the rest of his nobility. The King
made no reply except that Penn knew how to speak candidly, and that he gladly listened to him.

William Penn soon became known as a man to see if you
had business at Court. Around the Penn menage gathered a
crowd of clients and suppliants anxious to have him intercede
for them with the King. That he enjoyed his success is hardly
to his discredit. His ready acceptance of the role of courtier
could be regarded as an improvement over the flinty rigorism
of his earlier years. It was a pity his mother did not live to
see him come around to something approximating her point
of view, to see him as the "greate man" his father had tried
to make of him.

Throughout the reign Penn was an advisor of James, but an unofficial one. It was not with him that the King consulted when day-to-day decisions were being taken or formal notes drawn up. His influence has to be balanced against that of the men whose privilege it was to advise the King officially on domestic affairs and foreign policy.

Two of these men proved supremely efficacious in the shipwreck of the regime—the weak, incautious, optimistic Jesuit, Edward Petre, who, according to Barillon the French ambassador, "is very much in the King's confidence," and the sinister Earl of Sunderland, who "urged the king forward so rashly that some have thought he was deliberately planning his ruin." Petre and Sunderland, to whom James listened when his destiny was working itself out, gave him advice calculated to bring him a reputation for bigotry and dictatorial ambitions. The moderates fell by the wayside; the extremists he kept in power until events forced his eyes open at the end.

"James had at his side no good counsellor, and only one good man," according to Trevelyan. Since the "one good man" happened to be perhaps the best man in the kingdom, James cannot be condemned out of hand. He was consulting William Penn all the time, unofficially but none the less genuinely, raising for us the extremely complicated problem of how Penn was related to Petre and Sunderland at Whitehall. Penn left no written judgment of the latter two, even though they were so influential in laying out for the reign a route that diverged from the course he would have set. Conversely, we cannot go to either Petre or Sunderland for an opinion of Penn. We must try to clarify the situation by appealing to psychological probabilities.

Penn, Petre, Sunderland—they make an odd trio. With Petre, Penn had little to do, the Quaker and the Jesuit apparently not possessing much in common. If Penn felt the

incongruity of Petre's position at Court, he kept his opinion
to himself. Sunderland he had been acquainted with for many
years, had dealt with him when the Pennsylvania project was
in the making, and apparently trusted him as James did. In
one way Penn's attitude toward Sunderland was justified,
for the honesty of the one and the hypocrisy of the other
sometimes brought them to the same conclusion in practical
affairs : both defended the King's extravagant Catholic ob-
servances, Penn with sincerity, Sunderland with insincerity.

In another way these two pose a real enigma since, their
opinions conflicting at decisive moments, a struggle for the
King's ear ought to have broken out. Possibly it did. We
simply know too little that is incontrovertible about what was
said in the royal apartments when James II was alone with
Sunderland or Petre or Penn or anyone else. We know too
little about what these individuals said to one another, or how
they reacted to one another, when they met.

The fate of the Earl of Rochester would be very revealing,
if only Penn's view of it had been recorded. Rochester, un-
swervingly Anglican on the penal laws and the Test Act, was
given by James II, at the instigation of Sunderland, the choice
between conversion to Catholicism and the loss of his post at
the Treasury. Rochester preferred retirement.

It is true that James considered Rochester a potential convert, one who might change his religion if pushed to decide
as he would if he dared; and the King had this to go on, that
the Earl was willing to listen to both Catholic and Anglican
theologians before making up his mind. It is true that Sunderland came to fear that his rival might end by announcing
a genuine conversion. It is true also that James held Rochester
in high regard even while compelling him to a decision, and
that he rebuked Sunderland for implying that the feeling was
unwarranted : "In his alarm Sunderland was unwise enough
to insinuate to the King that Rochester might pretend to be

converted in order to gain time, only to receive the crushing reply that he knew Lord Rochester's character better than that."

These mitigating conditions surrounding the incident should not have satisfied William Penn, who could only have reacted to it on the basis of his moral theology, which would have informed him that James had no right to tamper thus with another man's conscience. Yet the method rather than the outcome would have disturbed him: he could have felt no dismay at the retirement of an opponent of complete religious toleration, and he did not question the King's right to choose agents who would advance the royal policies. He would have admired Rochester more for adhering to his faith than for adhering to the conviction that that faith ought to be dominant in England. Did Penn and James thrash the matter out in those terms? The question can be asked, but not answered.

"At this time the word 'closeting' comes into existence. It describes the negotiations of the King in his cabinet or 'closet' with the personages whose support he wished to gain for his object." Just so. The result is that for us documentary evidence is lacking too often; inference too often has to take its place.

A careful appraisal of the reign, common sense applied to what data there are, suggests that Penn and Sunderland alternated as influences moving James to action, with the Earl emerging ever more strongly at the end. Sunderland had, after all, a group to work with in persuading the King; Penn was but a lone figure standing out against them (although this balance of power indicates that Penn wielded enormous authority with James).

What about James himself? The probability is that he never saw a clear-cut issue before him. Penn and Sunderland were old acquaintances who would give him the same advice one day and contradictory advice the next. The King held his own views, opinions, purposes, schemes. And all the talk he heard, all the contrary and contradictory proposals coming in from the sources available to him, had somehow to be evaluated in the light of intractable political reality. A more astute ruler might have tripped. No one can marvel that differing interpretations of the reign were, and are, possible.

Penn realized that it was no plain case of black and white, truth and error, right and wrong. He himself must often have been confused about the decisions taken at Whitehall. It would be absurd to look to him for an outspoken stand on every policy. The salient thing is that he recognized and strove to ward off certain Sunderland-backed blunders that contributed materially to the insurrection against James II. Penn might have had his personal experience at Whitehall in mind when he said: "It is certain, princes ought to have great allowances made them for faults in government, since they see by other people's eyes, and hear by their ears; but ministers of state, their immediate confidants and instruments, have much to answer for, if, to gratify private passions, they misguide the prince to do public injury."

Granted that this opinion really was a reaction to what he had seen and heard, he did not mean to imply that James, however badly informed and by whomsoever, had been guilty of any radical "public injury." He considered the King a ruler human enough to have made mistakes but who was on the whole a good ruler deprived of his throne by a rally of the foolish mob behind interested traitors. Penn did not put it in quite so bellicose a form. That is, nonetheless, the moral behind his persistent public defense of James II.

5

PENN AS CENSOR
OF THE REIGN

WHEN PENN came forward as a public apologist for James II, he was no royal echo, nor could James have mistaken him for one. The record of Penn's anti-Stuart and anti-Catholic activities was too long and too well-known to be covered up. More, he did not renounce any part of it; and if he ceased to be guilty of such overt acts as championing Algernon Sidney at the polls, he in a very significant sense constituted himself a censor of the reign. That is, he would protest whenever he thought the King had blundered or tried to enforce his will beyond the limits allowed the moral law or the prerogative of the English monarchy.

Penn knew that the best way to gain the appreciation of James II was to profess conversion to Catholicism. Sunderland used the gambit and profited immensely. So did others around the Court. Penn, notwithstanding, remained staunchly Protestant. He would not disown the writings in which he had supported Quaker, and excoriated Catholic, doctrine. Unapologetic about his *Seasonable Caveat against Popery,* which had been in the public domain for fifteen years, he ceased to write so bitterly of Catholicism; but he expressed as usual his total disbelief in it.

A few months after James ascended the throne Penn wrote *Fiction Found Out* (1685), which indignantly denies the allegation of his being a crypto-Catholic. Having written the pamphlet, he proceeded to publish it—boldly and with the

King's full knowledge. The next year Penn took up the same subject in an exchange of letters with John Tillotson, a notable Anglican divine and later Archbishop of Canterbury. Again Penn protested that no one had any right to call him a Catholic, and his self-defense was genuine enough to bring an apology from Tillotson.

Penn's determination to shake off the Romanist label ought to have annoyed any Romanizing bigot; but James, as far as we know, took no offense at this insult to his religion. Penn remained very much the non-Catholic; he remained very much the courtier; and he still could depend on the King when it came to exercising the royal clemency with regard to persecuted Nonconformists.

Much the same held true in politics. His *England's Great Interest* (his pro-Sidney propaganda), Penn would not retract. He himself says that in 1684 (the year after Sidney's execution) he was "informed of for meeting with men of the Whig Stamp." If he had dropped his Whig friends when he entered the Court of James II, he would only have been discreet, diplomatic, perhaps justified.

He did no such thing. He went on dealing with the King's opponents. He became a partisan of notorious critics of the regime and won royal pardons for a number of them, including John Locke. Exiled in Holland, Locke rejected the clemency on the ground that he had done nothing wrong. The Court opinion was that he had done much wrong just by serving Shaftesbury. Yet James II, badgered by Penn, was prepared to let bygones be bygones.

The most remarkable case of Penn's political intercession concerned Aaron Smith, a man tarred with the brush of the Rye House Plot. Charlwood Lawton, who prevailed on Penn to act for Smith, quotes him to this effect: "I mentioned thy friend Aaron Smith's pardon this morning to the King, and he was never so angry with me in his life. He was ready to turn me out of his Closet, and said, six such men would put his three Kingdoms in a flame."

That, one would think, would close the matter for a wilful tyrant. Penn, however, returned to the attack later on, and finally wangled the Smith pardon.

Acting in behalf of James' critics came naturally to Penn, for he too was a critic. He did not have to go to others to be instructed about the mistakes of the reign. He saw them himself, nor would he remain silent about what he saw. He freely criticized James II; and his criticism of four fateful events of the reign — the Bloody Assize, Magdalen College, the drive to pack Parliament, and the Seven Bishops — has descended to us in print.

The Bloody Assize

James's willingness to have Whig adversaries go free was a noteworthy deference to Penn, for the King had had to face not merely vocal condemnation but conspiracy and even armed attack. The Rye House Plot had included him as an intended victim while he was still Duke of York, and shortly after his accession came the Monmouth Rebellion led by that natural son of Charles II whom Whigs like Shaftesbury had hoped to maneuver onto the throne by way of the Exclusion Bill.

One point customarily made against James II is the manner in which adherents of Monmouth were punished after the debacle in which the rising ended. To preside over their trials James sent Chief Justice Jeffreys, he of the Bloody Assize. Jeffreys dealt so harshly with the accused, browbeating and insulting them from the bench, then meting out the lash, jail, transportation and death, that his name has come down to us as one of the most infamous in the history of English law.

Whether or not the Bloody Assize actually went beyond the

penal practices of the time and caused bitter resentment among the people of England, how much the King really knew of what his Chief Justice was doing—problems like these are still matters of varying opinions among the historians. Later, after the Glorious Revolution, James and Jeffreys blamed one another. On James' side stands William Penn, who told Bishop Burnet that the Chief Justice was responsible for the brutalities: "He said to me, the king was much to be pitied, who was hurried into all this effusion of blood by Jeffreys's impetuous and cruel temper."

Presumably Penn was repeating his interpretation of the King's version of what had happened at the Bloody Assize. He obviously did not believe the worst construction placed on the King's maintenance of Jeffreys as presiding judge. But he did not therefore approve of the punishments, and he let James know how he felt: "About three hundred hanged in divers towns in the west, about one thousand to be transported. I begged twenty of the king."

This can only mean that in general James gave his sanction to the Bloody Assize, while remaining at the same time open to a review of special cases when his Quaker confidant brought them to his attention. It does not imply any wide divergence of opinion about the legalities. Penn would agree with James on the enormity of rebellion. He would understand the peculiar animosity that James felt toward the men implicated in this particular rebellion, for Monmouth had first tried to wrest the throne from him by political means, and, thwarted, had now turned to violence. Who could blame the King for feeling vindictive?

Penn, always charitable, may have put mercy above the law when James was rigorous for justice to the limit. Penn objected to the Bloody Assize for humanitarian reasons. James would have found it good politics had he followed

Penn's advice instead of allowing the law, as embodied in Jeffreys, to take its course.

Penn, however, apparently never urged mercy for the one man in whose case it would have been most prudent : he did not advise the King to spare Monmouth, who, alive and in the Tower, would have been an obstacle to the advance of William of Orange to the throne. With Monmouth executed, William, over in Holland, was able to reexamine his prospects with regard to England.

Macaulay, in his bid to shatter Penn's reputation, makes much of one sequel to Monmouth's rebellion — the affair of the Maids of Taunton. Some young girls who had been brought out to greet the rebel during his march were, after his failure, forced to buy pardons from the Queen's ladies-in-waiting. Macaulay makes Penn a party to the extortion :

> The maids of honor then requested William Penn to act for them ; and Penn accepted the commission. Yet it should seem that a little of the pertinacious scrupulosity which he had often shown about taking off his hat would not have been altogether out of place on this occasion. He probably silenced the remonstrances of his conscience by repeating to himself that none of the money which he extorted would go into his own pocket ; that if he refused to be the agent of the ladies they would find agents less humane ; that by complying he should increase his influence at the court; and that his influence at the court had already enabled him, and might still enable him, to render great services to his oppressed brethren.

Penn's admirers have not allowed Macaulay's allegation to pass. They point out that he invoked as his sole piece of evidence a letter written by Sunderland, and one that seems to have been addressed not to William Penn but to a certain George Penne. Penn's leading defender therefore declares Macaulay guilty of misusing the evidence, of mistaking an

"unwarrantable assumption" for historical fact. No one has
overturned this verdict.

Magdalen College

If the Bloody Assizze did not provoke any real protest
during James's reign, the case of Magdalen College, Oxford,
did. James intended to help his co-religionists in various ways,
one of which was to force their acceptance by the universities.
Therefore, when the President of Magdalen died, the King
decided to impose a Catholic successor on the Fellows of the
College. He ordered them to set aside their preference in
favor of his, and caused the expulsion of those who refused.

This assault on a great educational foundation of a tra-
ditionally Royalist university was, if not instigated, at least
backed and handled by the Sunderland clique at Court.
Indeed, Sunderland himself almost certainly misled the King
by withholding a petition from the Fellows of Magdalen at
one critical juncture and then sending an abrupt rejection in
the King's name. The two Fellows who bore the petition to
Court, Francis Bagshaw and Thomas Smith, could not get
past Sunderland. Later when James told the Vice-Chancellor
that the Fellows should have appealed to the Crown before
proceeding to their election, Smith commented: "This
seemed demonstration that the Earl of Sunderland did not
deliver our petition in good time. . . ." It was not the only
occasion on which Sunderland roused suspicion by his handling of letters intended for the King.

Some scholars have seen Sunderland and Petre as co-
conspirators; others have considered Petre the senior partner
in the duplicity that forced James farther and faster than he
would have gone of his own free will. However that may be,
James never disavowed any part of Sunderland's tactics with
the college, much less made any move to get rid of him for

insubordination until the regime was toppling. The King felt that, whether or not a strong stand at the start had been justified, he could not afford to back down once committed to the Sunderland policy. He followed that policy to the end and was discredited by it.

James II blundered on Magdalen College. Did William Penn help him to blunder? Macaulay, as might be expected, finds that he did. He pictures Penn as strictly the King's man throughout the embroglio, using bribes and threats to make the Fellows of Magdalen give in: "The courtly Quaker, therefore, did his best to seduce the college from the path of right."

This time there is no question of the verdict that must be passed on the historian. Magdalen College reveals Penn, not as the King's man, but in his capacity of censor of the reign. It is one more example of his readiness to criticize James II. There is no need to follow the turns and twists through which the affair wound to its conclusion: the truth has been familiar enough ever since the critics began to test Macaulay's knowledge against the documentary evidence. In sum, we know that Penn realized the King was wrong, morally, legally, and prudentially, about Magdalen College, and that he had the courage to tell him so. A non-Quaker expert on both Macaulay and the history of England in the seventeenth century puts the standard rejoinder in these words: "An examination of the evidence shows that Penn was concerned in the affair as the agent of the college rather than of the King. He interceded with the King on behalf of the college, and that not once but twice over. Far from trying to persuade the Fellows to give way he wrote to James that 'in their circumstances, they could not yield obedience without a breach of their oaths.' "

A Quaker scholar is less restrained in his rebuttal and speaks of "Mr. Macaulay's perversions and omissions." The

single substantial verity left in the relevant pages of the
History of England is that Penn did believe with the King
that Catholics had a right to attend Oxford and to hold office
in the university, the same right as the Quakers and all other
non-Anglicans who were barred. He gave the King sane
advice, unavailing advice, about the privilege of the Fellows
of Magdalen to elect their own President. He agreed with
the King about the wider principle that no religious tests
should be levied on students at either Oxford or Cambridge.

The Drive to Pack Parliament

The point at which James II ought to have paused for a
serious reappraisal of the Sunderland approach concerned
the body of representatives who would have sat as James'
second Parliament, had his reign endured that long. He
conceived the idea, and Sunderland did nothing to disturb it,
of marshaling a compliant legislature by manipulating the
elections.

> With this object in view, the remodelling of the corpora-
> tions was carried still further, and Roman Catholics and
> Dissenters were admitted to those boroughs which returned
> members to Parliament ; Roman Catholics were appointed
> as lords-lieutenant in the counties ; and three questions
> were propounded to the deputy-lieutenants and the justices
> of the peace : (1) Whether, if chosen to serve in Parliament,
> you will consent to the repeal of the penal laws and the
> Test Act ? (2) Whether, if not standing yourself, you will
> vote for a member who will do so ? (3) Whether you will
> be willing to maintain the Declaration of Indulgence ?

High-handedly interfering in local districts already suspicious of him, trying to force presiding officials to see to the
defeat of unsatisfactory candidates, James paid for his mis-
calculation by suffering a series of rebuffs and by increasing

animosity in quarters that not even a reigning sovereign could hector with impunity.

Penn was in two minds about the drive to pack Parliament. He knew as well as anyone that the House of Commons was no democratic voice of all the people, but rather the carefully-guarded preserve of the nation's vested interests; and when speaking publicly he backs the King, who "seems to me to be Unpacking for the Good of the Whole that which hath been so long Packt for the Good of a Party." The men whom James wanted to have in Parliament (those favorable to universal religious freedom) were mainly those Penn would have preferred. In previous elections Penn had concentrated on the rights of Parliament as an institution of the English realm. Now he was concentrating on the crimes of Parliament as a closed corporation of magnates and bishops.

Penn, nonetheless, protested to the King against the manipulation of the coming election. His political philosophy was at stake; for he believed that, in the abstract, electors should not be coerced. Perhaps he would have been willing to let his principle slide into abeyance for the sake of an attainable good—a Parliament favorable to religious liberty—but that this could in fact be attained by the King's interference began to seem increasingly dubious. Penn felt the swelling tide of resentment, much of it false and unwarranted in his estimation, but no less dangerous for all that. Not only did he warn James in urgent terms not to force the Parliamentary issue, but he gathered factual material to bolster his warning, evidence of fear and hostility among people of power throughout the country. He even brought to the palace Whig and Anglican spokesmen who, at his advice, insisted on their loyalty to the Crown, to James II, even while frankly confessing that they were bound to oppose tampering with elections or undermining the position of the Church of England.

One of these spokesmen was Charlwood Lawton, whose memoir remains an invaluable witness to Penn's activities at Whitehall. Penn prompted Lawton to speak his mind without hesitation, and then introduced him to the King. Knowing that, even so, the subject would hold back his strongest opinions while addressing his sovereign, Penn got around Lawton's diffidence by asking him to send him unsigned criticisms of the state of the kingdom. "That, and several other Anonymous Letters which he, by honest artifice, from time to time, got from me, he showed to the King, but never would let His Majesty know who wrote them. . . The King, however, had, from time to time, my thoughts in the many invective anonymous Letters, which, with so good a Design, Mr. Penn drew from me upon every occasion."

Lawton's hatred of "regulated Parliaments" manifests itself in the conversations recorded in his memoir. How much more vigorously must it have glowed in the writings that he knew would never be traced to him! James, so far from resenting Lawton's attitude, said he "liked me for my sincerity," and offered him royal backing should he volunteer to run for Parliament—surely an astonishing invitation, granted that the King *was* an ambitious autocrat intolerant of opposition.

That James was acting out of character might possibly be argued if Lawton's and Penn's testimony were all we had to go on. We have, however, at least one corroboratory witness who deserves to be heard before the case is closed. The King asked the Earl of Abingdon to help him maneuver suitable candidates into Parliament. Abingdon in response

desired his Majesty to consider how unfit any man was to be a solicitor in a cause that was against his own judgment? His Majesty said he was sorry it was so; for he had made a resolution not to keep any one in his service, who would not serve him in all things ; to which I replied that I took *It* (the Commission) for his brother's and his service, and hoped he was satisfied that I had managed it so, and when he thought anyone could do it better, I should be very willing to part with it. He said he was fully satisfied therewith, and that he always thought me a person of worth and honour, and that I had dealt with him in this business like one.

James could have been under no illusion about the possibility of "using" Charlwood Lawton or the Earl of Abingdon. That he was "using" William Penn would by now appear to be at least as questionable. And we are not yet finished with Penn as censor of the reign.

The Seven Bishops

The last major case in which we know that Penn expostulated with James II was that of the Seven Bishops. In 1688 James issued his second Declaration of Indulgence, announced that Parliament (the packed Parliament he was struggling to achieve) would convene again and vote on the measure, and commanded the bishops of his kingdom to have the Declaration read throughout their dioceses. Seven Anglican ecclesiastics, led by the Archbishop of Canterbury, petitioned the King to recall the order; they said that the dispensing power by which James set aside laws passed in Parliament was illegal. In reply, he prosecuted the bishops for seditious libel.

During his exile in France, James named Jeffreys as the one who urged him to bring the bishops into court; and it seems clear that he must have consulted his top legal advisor about the possibility of obtaining a conviction. The evidence concerning Sunderland and Petre is confusing. Barillon says they wanted the affair dropped; but it is easier to believe the French ambassador mistaken than to believe that James had no support from them, especially since he was being exhorted by William Penn to retreat as gracefully as possible.

Penn was dead set against the prosecution. Whatever the law might say, he regarded it as a violation of conscience to give men of the cloth such a command. He dreaded the explosion that would follow should James thrust a match into the powder keg that was Whig and Anglican England. He recognized the dilemma posed by an otherwise happy event of the moment, the birth of a son to the Queen, which to the antagonists of James II meant just one thing : they could gain nothing by waiting for their Catholic monarch to die since he would be followed by his Catholic heir. Charlwood Lawton has left us a picture of Penn at the climactic moment in 1688.

> Before I go further, I must set down Mr. Penn's own behaviour, that Summer, in relation to the Bishops who were sent to the Tower. He was not only against their Commitment ; but, the day the Prince of Wales was born, he went to the King and pressed him exceedingly to set them at liberty, and to order, in Council, a General Pardon to be issued out, as soon as it could pass the Seals. He pressed most heartily to have both done, and told His Majesty, that, on that happy Day, every body ought to rejoice, which they would do, if the Bishops were let out ; and it was generally known that such a Pardon would soon be proclaimed. Mr. Penn hoped the occasion would have made him succeed in both Proposals ; and I suppose all men must own, it was unhappy for the King that he did not follow Mr. Penn's advice. But there were about the King some villainous Knaves, and others who were as visionary fools (I can't help calling them so), who set themselves against every wise measure that was laid before that unfortunate Prince, either by Mr. Penn, or any body else ; and they overpersuaded the King not to lay hold of so good an opportunity to regain the affections of multitudes of his People, who were justly startled, and much provoked,

by seeing the right reverend Fathers of the Church illegally committed to prison.

No one has ever improved on this description of Penn confronting James II when the throne of England lay as a prize to be won or lost depending on how the political game went. It speaks well for Penn's practical sagacity that, in the heat of the hour when passions were becoming more furious on every side, he divined precisely how the situation might be retrieved. The Seven Bishops were in the Tower of London; the Queen had just presented the King with an heir to the throne—mischievous developments both, as far as the Anglicans and Whigs were concerned. But just because they happened together, they might be used together to counteract the fears so widely spread in the country: let the King but release the bishops as a grace due to the birth of his son, and the birth and the imprisonment might neutralize each other instead of reinforcing each other.

James refused to listen. It is impossible to say whether he was himself the prime mover or whether he was hurried on by the Sunderland junto—Lawton's "villainous Knaves" and "visionary fools." In any case, James forced the trial of the Seven Bishops to its predestinate end; and when the verdict of "not guilty" came in from the jury, the throne rocked. Then, in short order, the invitation to William of Orange, followed by his successful invasion of England, the exile of James II, and the ruin of the Stuart dynasty. Thenceforth James II and his son and his grandson belong to the history, not of the government of England, but of the Jacobite movement.

Summing Up

Throughout, the impression we get of William Penn is of a good friend and unofficial advisor of the King, close enough to express his disapproval, frankly and forcefully, at what he takes to be missteps on the part of his sovereign, but in no position to speak as one formally bound by an office to do so. Much of the pressure he exerted was indirect, as with the anonymous letters he solicited from Charlwood Lawton and like-minded men in order to keep James aware of the pitfalls along the way. Toward the end Penn strove ever more urgently to make the King understand that his ends, of which Penn usually approved, could not be achieved by the means adopted, that the ends were really jeopardized by the means.

The impression we get of James II is of a monarch who too often allowed an insidious counter-force (Sunderland, Petre, Jeffreys) to drive him toward the harshest means suggested to him by his native inclinations. Penn opposed the worst side of James; the others nurtured it; and therein lay half the explanation of what happened.

During the last year of his reign James Stuart seemed bent on raising imprudence to the level of an heroic vice. He hardened his worst enemies in their disaffection. He alienated followers who would have stayed with him under conditions less onerous to themselves. And he did it knowing full well that the ranks closed against him had acknowledged a leader in his Dutch rival.

William Penn, nevertheless, remained loyal. At no time did he lose his faith in James II or so much as consider abandoning him. He was sure in his own mind that James, his evident and sometimes crass errors notwithstanding, remained an essentially good ruler and by all odds the best of the alternatives available to the people of England. Penn the censor of the reign continued to be heard; but so did Penn the eulogist of the reign. He did not recognize any ambivalence within himself, any split personality with regard to James. Let us try to see why.

6

PENN, JAMES
AND CATHOLICISM

THE ROYAL acts which Penn tried to dissuade James from committing do not in themselves support a very formidable indictment of the King. Magdalen College was a real misdemeanor, supplemented as it was by James' effort to push Catholics into other places held by Anglicans. But the moralities and legalities of both the Bloody Assize and the trial of the Seven Bishops remain ambiguous. The drive to pack Parliament was no novelty, nor was it by any means the last thing of its kind; and Penn's wavering but reflected the confusion that must result from any honest look at the manner in which both sides behaved in elections.

Another sovereign might have survived such blunders. What caused the furor was James' religion. He was a Catholic ruler of a predominantly Protestant people, and a people who regarded their Protestantism as inseparably bound up with their nationality. They were easily aroused by the slightest suspicion of a Romanizing tendency. However much Anglicans and Dissenters might dispute with one another, they were at least one in their hatred of Rome.

Charles II had understood the psychological state of his subjects. He did all he could to convince them that he interpreted his duties as King to include loyal leadership of the Church of England, opposition to the Church of Rome, and a determination to control the conduct of English Catholics. The terror of the Popish Plot persuaded him of the correctness of his judgment, for here was an example of Catholics being savagely assailed on the basis of obvious falsehoods.

James II took a very different view of the crisis. He thought Charles should have been more courageous about intervening to save the victims and that the caution of his brother merely exacerbated the whole thing. He himself would know better how to behave as King of England and as an English Catholic.

His theory that boldness was called for was his first mistake. Allied with it was his persistent inability to understand the logic of the religious division of his kingdom. He took High Churchmen to be close to, and ready for, the final step into Catholicism; they were not. He believed that the Anglicans generally would stand by their traditional policy of non-resistance to the Crown; he believed it just when they had reached the stage of scrapping non-resistance. Angry about the mistreatment of English Catholics, remembering the Popish Plot, he could not realize how fierce the majority of his subjects were because of their folk memory of Mary Tudor and the Gunpowder Plot.

His coronation hardly over, James gave his enemies a handle to use against him. He began to parade his Catholicism. He heard Mass openly at Court and tried to lure his Anglican courtiers into accompanying him. He encouraged diffident Catholics to come out of hiding, rewarded converts, and acknowledged a Papal nuncio. He began to appoint Catholics to posts in the government and the army, dispensing with the Test Act to do so—that is, waiving the Parliamentary law that such places should be reserved to men who would take the oath against the religion of Rome. He appointed a Court of High Commission to supervise Anglican affairs since he himself could not perform the duties of head of the Church of England, a procedure that seemed more reasonable to him than it did to the Anglicans.

The King's overt, not to say blatant, profession and practice of his Catholic faith alarmed a mass of Englishmen, and
started some of them to thinking more seriously about the
fact that there were other candidates for the throne beside
James Stuart. This explains the amount of support the Duke
of Monmouth ("the Protestant Duke") received, and the increasing favor, following his defeat, that the Calvinist
William of Orange inherited.

William Penn was one Englishman who felt no apprehension about the King's religion. In a letter surviving from
these early months of the reign he remarks noncommittally :
"The Popish lords and gentry go to Whitehall to mass daily,
and the Tower, or Royal Chapel is crammed by vying with
the Protestant lords and gentry." Instead of being jolted
by the spectacle, Penn moved to the other extreme and
defended the change around Whitehall as another piece of
evidence for the straightforwardness of James II — a change
to be praised rather than censured, as he himself informed
the King : "He declared he concealed himself to obey his
brother, and that now he would be above-board; which we
like the better on many accounts. I was with him and told
him so; but, withal, hoped we should come in for a share.
He smiled, and said he desired not that a peaceable people
should be disturbed for their religion."

Penn's attitude was characteristic. He wanted everyone to
go to church or meeting house openly and without fear, and
he did not except the Catholics, not even the Catholics at
Whitehall. In advising James, nevertheless, Penn very possibly made a bad misjudgment. If it was fair enough that he
should prefer a frank profession of one's true belief even (or
especially) in a king, yet he might have tempered his enthusiasm by observing the impolitic way it was done by James II
who, not satisfied merely with a declaration of his creed, had
to make an exaggerated display of it in the teeth of a fearful

and dangerous opposition. Penn recalled the devious be-
haviour of Charles II, in whom he disliked the unmanly
refusal to be candid about his religion until he lay on his
deathbed, and was happy to recognize in James an attitude
closer to the Quaker concept of truthfulness. James probably
was thinking more about the political effect of his Catholicism, which he believed would be favorable to him. Penn was
thinking more about the moral implications. Their different
approaches brought them to the same conclusion.

Penn's advice to James to go ahead would have been better
adapted to Charles. Being the reverse of that monarch's self-
indulgent inclinations, it might have exerted a salutary pressure toward moderation, toward less pretence about religion.
With James, Penn's advice ran in the same direction as the
royal will; it did nothing to deter the King from the intem-
perate conduct that ruined him.

As the reign moved on to its tragic climax Penn may have
become more reserved in his approval of the King's profession
of faith. He would not, all the same, have conceded much. He
completely agreed with the fundamentals by which James
worked. He felt that the King had a perfect right to do something for the Catholics and a human right to the exasperation
that would redress the balance by humiliating their persecutors. This, after all, and allowing for Penn's less vindictive
nature, was not very different than what he himself had in
mind for the Quakers.

Penn, thinking how the Friends had been singled out for
oppression by the Quakers' Act, could not forget that the Test
Act was aimed directly at the Catholics. He knew that his
own patrimony had been threatened by his religious faith
and that the royal patrimony of the King had for the same
reason been threatened much more. He recalled that James
Stuart had been marked for personal contumely by the
Exclusion Bill, the purpose of which was to bar him from the

throne and give it to the bastard Duke of Monmouth. If the Exclusion Bill was an insult to the legitimate heir to the throne, the Test Act was an injury to him, just as it was to Penn and the members of the Society of Friends.

Is the Quaker's allegiance to the Catholic, then, so difficult to understand? Is there any genuine problem why Penn wrote: "Pardon me, we have not to do with an insensible Prince, but one that has been touched with our Infirmities: More than any Body, fit to Judge our Cause, by the share he once had in it. Who should give Ease like the Prince that has wanted it?"

When James went on from flourishing his Catholicism like a flag to the appointment of Catholics to office, Penn still had no protest to make. If he considered that James acted too cavalierly, and it would have been no compromise of his principles had he done so, still he held nothing against the Catholics as such; rather was he pleased to see the Test Act lifted from their shoulders—and from the Quakers too. The question of military leadership reveals a unanimity between monarch and subject. James "owned that there were officers in this army who had not taken the tests, and he said that, in view of their past services and of possible future needs, he intended to keep them." Penn, in advocating this same argument from practical prudence, goes to a reminiscence about his father's naval career: "I do very well remember he presented our present King with a catalogue of the knowingest and bravest officers the age had bred, with this subscribed, 'These men, if his Majesty will please to admit of their Persuasions, I will answer for their skill, courage and integrity.' He picked them by their Ability, not their Opinions; and he was in the right; for that was the best way of doing the King's business."

In 1687 the King decided to get rid of the Test Act Act altogether instead of merely waiving it occasionally in individual cases. He promulgated his first Declaration of Indulgence. William Penn has ever since been accused of having a hand in this, and the accusation is just. The Declaration of Indulgence was the masterpiece wrought by him as unofficial advisor to James II. No one knows whether he actually wrote the document or any part of it, but several clauses echo his thought if not his words, for instance the one that declares religious freedom and security of property to be "the two things men value most. . . ."

The measure separated an Englishman's religion from his nationality, made hypocrisy and false conversion unnecessary except for toadies at Court, and incidentally brought the Quakers into full citizenship for the first time. It therefore encapsulated the main items to achieve which Penn had labored for so long.

The Quakers were peculiarly gratified by the King's announcement. They were among the first to express their appreciation for the mercy extended to them by the King through the Declaration of Indulgence. William Penn led a delegation of Friends to Whitehall to offer a formal statement of esteem and thanks, the members of the delegation being so moved that they left their hats outside when they were admitted to the audience chamber. In his opening remarks Penn extolled James for his magnanimity.

By this Grace He has relieved his Distressed Subjects from their Cruel Sufferings, and raised to Himself a New and Lasting Empire by adding their Affection to their Duty. And we pray God to continue the King in this Noble Resolution; for He is now upon a Principle that has Good Nature, Christianity, and the Good of Civil Society on its Side, a Security to Him beyond the Little Arts of Government. I would not that any should think that we came hither with Design to fill the *Gazette* with our Thanks, but as our sufferings would have moved Stones to Compassion, so we should be harder if we were not moved to Gratitude.

Penn then read the Quaker address to the throne, thanking the King with the usual rhetoric, and adding the hope that Parliament might set its seal of approval on the royal act that allowed freedom of conscience to all Englishmen.

James replied with the words: "Gentlemen, I thank you heartily for your Address. Some of you know (I am sure you do, Mr. Penn) that it was always my Principle, That Consciences ought not to be forced, and that all men ought to have the Liberty of their Consciences. And what I have promis'd in my Declaration I will continue to perform as long as I live. And I hope, before I die, to settle it so that After Ages shall have no Reason to alter it."

The King's Prerogative

Both sides at this meeting had in mind Parliamentary concurrence with the Declaration of Indulgence. Both looked to the legislature to ratify what the King had done. But had James any right thus to remove the Test Act? Was his Declaration of Indulgence legal?

From the enemies of the Court there welled up a flood of protests. They insisted that an act of Parliament should stand until repealed in Parliament. They called in question the dispensing, and a fortiori the suspending, powers of the Crown. The Marquis of Halifax took the lead with his *Letter to a Dissenter* (1687) in which he admonished the sects not to be deceived about the intentions of the King and the Catholics around him and not to accept an illegality that contravened Parliamentary legislation.

Halifax spoke for all those Englishmen who distrusted James II. By publicizing his own fears in a forceful polemical pamphlet, he played on the fears that existed in certain quarters throughout the country. To him as much as to any

single man was due the formulation, solidification, and per-
petuation of the thesis that those Dissenters who were satisfied
with relief through the Declaration of Indulgence, through
an arbitrary act of the Crown, were purblind fools who for
the sake of a temporary respite jeopardized their future with
an oppression more severe than any they had yet experienced.
Believing that the King's overruling of the Test Act was un-
lawful, Halifax made many others believe it too.

William Penn did *not* believe it. He regarded this use of the
royal prerogative as right in theory and necessary under the
existing circumstances. He thought the Dissenters were sensible when they accepted the boon for what it was, short-
sighted and ungrateful when they grumbled about the
channel through which religious freedom reached them.

To puzzzle over how Penn could have approved James'
use of the dispensing and suspending powers of the Crown
is to fall into *the* pseudo-problem of Penn scholarship. For
him the question was not the ultimate source of political
authority in England : it was not a case of being for King or
Parliament. It was a case of being for or against the natural
law.

Nothing would be less profitable than trying to run down
the sources on which Penn drew for this part of his political
philosophy. He himself could not have sorted them out. The
theory of natural law permeated the intellectual atmosphere
around him; it was in half the books he read; he could have
heard of it from dozens of men whose paths crossed his when
his thought was still in its formative stage. He had read
Aristotle and St. Augustine and Grotius. He had studied with
John Owen and Moses Amyraut. Moreover, he had met, and
rejected, the opposite theory : he deliberately turned away
from Hobbes and the notion that the state creates right.

To believe in the natural law does not necessarily lead
political philosophers to the same conclusions. John Locke

began with the usual premise about objective truth, goodness
and duty, but he did not end up, as did William Penn, by
believing in the right of Catholics to share in the full life of
the state. Penn's concept of the natural law must be interpreted above all with reference to theology. He thought it an
objective truth, beyond impeachment by any human being or
any group, that all men receive divine inspiration through
the Inner Light and that all are commanded to follow the
teaching of this spiritual mentor. He made his point in
technical philosophical language when speaking of the impact
of inspiration on conduct : "It is the first Lesson of the great
Synteresis, so much renowned by the Philosophers and
Civilians, learns Mankind to do as one would be done to."
That is, we know our duty naturally, and have a natural
right to do it.

From Penn's natural law premise is deducible a whole
corpus of political rules best summarized in two slogans of
which he never heard : Life, Liberty and the Pursuit of
Happiness; and Liberty, Equality and Fraternity. Before
Locke, he accepted the traditional theory that property is
guaranteed by rights derived from a supra-human source,
both liberty and property being sacrosanct under "the great
Charters of Nature and Scripture."

Penn further defended the rights of man by an extension
of the natural law called the law of nations. A Roman legal
principle based on the cosmopolitan political philosophy of
the Greek Stoics, the law of nations told him that there is a
norm of international morality (analogous to national morality) by which independent states are bound in their dealings
with one another, a morality of right and justice that always
exists regardless of how often it may be violated. Grotius,
arguing from Greek, medieval, and modern theory, had
written extensively of the law of nations. Penn added his bit

when he produced *An Essay towards the Present and Future Peace of Europe* (1693).

Penn had once used the law of nations as a weapon against James when he was Duke of York, writing during the negotiations over West Jersey: "For under favour we buy nothing of the duke, if not the right of an undisturbed colonizing, and that as Englishmen, with no diminution, but expectation of some increase, of those freedoms and privileges enjoyed in our own country; for the soil is none of his, 'tis the natives' by the *jus gentium*, by the laws of nations, and it would be an ill argument to convert to Christianity, to expel instead of purchasing them out of those countries."

Penn would allege the natural law even against his royal benefactor, even in behalf of aborigines living in a stone age culture. James did not object to the theory at the time; now, as King, he would profit from the theory. Penn invoked it as a defense of the Crown's prerogative.

He looked at the Test Act from the vantage ground of his principles of natural law, found the enactment to be a violation of justice, and concluded that it was in fact no true law at all, no matter what institutional authority might be behind it. *His* question was simply this: Who is violating the higher law, and who is defending it? The answer was not dubitable. Parliament had passed the Test Act; the King had set it aside; and to accuse the latter of acting illegally was to turn upside-down the system of objective values built into the structure of the universe and revealed to men by the Inner Light. (Since Penn, while tolerating all creeds, would restrict offices to professing Christians, there is an illogicality in his theology of the Inner Light; but the point is irrelevant to the practical politics in which he was engaged).

As Penn saw it, the real difficulty was to get the members of Parliament to stop infringing the natural law insofar as it inculcated freedom of conscience. Like James II, he hoped

for the election of a legislature that would abolish the Test
Act. Like the Whigs, he could not feel easy about any measure
that did not have Parliamentary approval. But until the legislators should come to their senses and do their duty, he was
all for the King doing his own duty and showing them the
way.

The idea that Penn allowed himself to be duped when he
defended the prerogative is manifestly unsound. It would be
much truer, would indeed be true without qualification, to
say that had he attacked the suspending power of the Crown
at the time of the Declaration of Indulgence, he would have
been false to the political philosophy that he had been advocating in different contexts over the years. Had he been persuaded by Halifax's *Letter to a Dissenter,* he would have had
to take back a mass of letters, pamphlets, books, public
declarations, and private remarks. In sheer consistency, if
nothing else, he had to accept the Declaration of Indulgence.
The sphere of his ideas cannot be shown to be without self-
contradictions; but he was never guilty of so crass a sophism
as holding, in defiance of his past attitudes, for the authority
of Parliament to override a precept of the natural law.

Penn's Theory of Religious Toleration

The idea that the working of the Inner Light must not be
hindered in the case of the individual has obvious implications for practical politics. The first of Penn's positive affirma-
tions is that believers, as long as they are law-abiding folk,
have a divine sanction to meet for worship. The right to
corporate gathering is the real test since conscience itself,
faith, belief, cannot be controlled from the outside. You cannot force a religious tenet into a man's mind, and to that
extent he is always free; you can, if you have the strength,
prevent him from meeting with his co-religionists, which

means that deliberately not to do so is the nub of any sound definition of religious toleration.

First, By Liberty of Conscience we understand not only a mere Liberty of the Mind in believing or disbelieving this or that Principle of Doctrine, but the exercise of ourselves in a visible Way of Worship upon our believing it to be indispensably required at our hands, that if we neglect it for Fear or Favour of any Mortal Man we sin and incur divine Wrath. . . .

Secondly, by Imposition, Restraining, and Persecution we don't only mean the strict requiring of us to believe this to be True or that to be False, and, upon Refusal, to incur the Penalties enacted in such Cases, but by those Terms we mean thus much : any coercive Let or Hindrance to us from meeting together to perform those religious Exercises which are according to our Faith and Persuasion.

The Test Act and the penal laws were such a "coercive Let or Hindrance" — to the Catholics, to the Quakers, to non-Anglicans in general. They were, to focus the argument on our two personalities, a violation of the natural religious rights of James Stuart and William Penn. Penn would never admit that sound divinity is to be found in acts of Parliament or judicial decisions under the common law or even the creeds of ecclesiastical councils; he thought always in terms of the individual conscience expanding in the healing rays of the Inner Light.

Penn was not so simple-minded as to believe that his theological arguments would win religious freedom for all Englishmen. He had more empirical, philosophical, and prudential motives to go on. He rang the changes on them in a succession of works from near the beginning of his writing career to near its end.

He united ethics and politics when he expatiated on distributive justice, the equitable sharing of rights and privileges (and duties and burdens) among the population. Distributive

justice favors the sectarians because they make part of the
state, and so have a claim to be sheltered by it : "If we are
contributaries to the maintenance of it, we are entitled to a
protection from it." This was a cardinal thought with the
Friends of the Penn era. As much as any other group, given
their numbers, they contributed to the prosperity of England.
Their religion taught them to be industrious, and they *were*
industrious wherever they were allowed to labor at their
tasks in peace. Penn was not the only one to call it abominable
that these reliable props of the English nation should be
harried for their pains. Unlike most observers, he extended his
principle to include all the religions, including the Catholic.

After the ethics of toleration, the prudence of toleration.
Penn would now prove that the persecutors themselves have
something to gain from the disappearance of the Test Act.
In brief, he considered intolerance as self-contradictory, raising up more difficulties for the government than it ever got
rid of.

Fundamentally, intolerance cannot achieve its purpose, for
the attempt to control spiritual acts with material reins is
futile. "To Conclude, there ought to be an Adequation and
Resemblance betwix all Ends and the Means to them, but in
this case there can be none imaginable; the End is the conformity of our Judgments and Understandings to the acts
of such as require it; the Means are Fines and Imprisonments
and bloody Knocks to boot. Now what Proportion or Assim-
ilation these bear, let the sober judge."

At this point, Penn's reasoning was undeniably defective.
Even as he wrote, Catholicism was receding in England precisely because the government had made the path so stony
for the Catholics. No doubt a Catholic would not be persuaded by the Test Act that the Church of England held the
key to the truth; but if, under the penalty of ruinous fines and
social ostracism, a Catholic parent should bend far enough to

send his children to Anglican schools and churches, then those children would very likely grow up to be believing Anglicans. Penn himself could easily have found such cases, had he gone looking for them. (He could have found them also among his own Quakers). The effectiveness of the penal laws was the one big point in their favor : they worked, and by the eighteenth century had made of England an over-whelmingly Protestant nation.

What is true, however, is that Parliamentary enactments never did produce an entirely Anglican England. The Dis-senters survived, and so vigorously that in the nineteenth century the penal laws were finally withdrawn. The sects survived because they were not hated as bitterly as the Catholics : the pressure to conform never weighed on them so intolerably. They came through the era of intolerance as a strong minority, the Catholics as a small harassed minority.

Penn was so anxious to convince the Anglicans that toler-ation is more prudential than intolerance that he pushed his argument to invalid limits, even though there is almost always some truth in what he says. It was right enough for him to assert that intolerance can cause civil disturbances; but he should have noted that brutality often produces civil unity, as when Louis XIV revoked the Edict of Nantes. Penn assumed too close a coincidence between morality and pru-dence in politics, although his exaggeration seems like truth itself compared to what the proponents of the penal laws were saying about the need of intolerance for reasons of state.

Penn did not make the mistake of calling for universal toleration. He knew that some things are intolerable and are not tolerated by civilized governments. If he was willing to allow any kind of faith, that was only as long as basic Christian ethics and conduct remain uncontaminated. Of religious toleration he remarked : "I did maintain it in favour of those that kept within the Bounds of Morality." And he

constricted "the Bounds of Morality" rather severely. No
theocrat in politics, he was no latitudinarian in religion, no
antinomian in ethics. He would have not merely criminals
but adulterers and even drunkards rooted out of society, and
he demanded that princes and governors give their subjects
a model of chastity and industry—an idea that must have
appeared more appropriate to James II than it had to Charles
II. Penn would not have magistrates turn a blind eye to the
vices of society.

Be pleased to consider your Commission, and examine the
Extent of your Authority. You will find that God and the
Government have impowered you to punish these impieties,
and it is so far from being a Crime that it is your Duty.
This is not troubling Men for Faith, nor perplexing People
for Tenderness of Conscience; there can be no pretence
to be Drunk, to Whore, to be Voluptuous, to Game, to
Swear, Curse, Blaspheme and Prophane ; no such Matter.
These are Sins against Nature and against Government as
well as against the Written Laws of God. They lay the
Axe to the Root of Human Society, and are the Common
Enemies of Mankind. 'Twas to prevent these Enormities
that Government was instituted ; and shall Government
indulge that which it is instituted to protect ?

Penn had too much good sense to push his theology of
individual inspiration to its logical end. He knew about
antinomianism, the claim of the individual to behave in any
way, even in the most outrageous, because he was following
the dictates of his Inner Light. It was an old story in the
history of theology and had once troubled Quakerism. Penn
opposed antinomianism on two grounds : it offends against
morality and Scripture, and it threatens the state.

He did not, therefore, take the line that Parliament is
never to interfere with the conduct of the citizenry. He did
take the line that the Test Act passed in Parliament was no
palladium of virtuous civic life, but rather an attack on faith,

on the Inner Light, on the natural law — and consequently something to be opposed for both religious and political reasons. James II, in Penn's opinion, had much more than the right to declare the Test Act null and void. He had the duty to do so.

The Toleration of Catholics

The furious controversy surrounding the Declaration of Indulgence really had little to do with law or politics. The prerogative of the Crown would scarcely have been called in question over legal or political technicalities, and James II certainly would never have lost his throne because of them. If the Seven Bishops couched their case in legal terms, their true motive was religious : they would not have the Declaration of Indulgence read in their dioceses because they would not see the Catholics relieved of their civil disabilities. If Halifax wrote scathingly of the suspending power, that was because it was being exercised in behalf of Catholics.

Even the most prominent libertarians tended to make an exception of Catholicism when calling for religious toleration. Before William Penn, John Milton had defended freedom of conscience, but not for Catholics. After Penn, John Locke defended the same freedom, but again not for Catholics. The reservation seemed so fitting to so many prominent Englishmen that neither Milton nor Locke ever suffered in reputation for making it.

Penn, of course, knew all about the reservation. He had read as thoroughly in the polemical literature as almost any man of his time, for he had to have all the arguments in favor of intolerance in mind while defending toleration. He was familiar with the current charges leveled against the Church of Rome. He was sincerely concerned both for England and for Protestantism. He might have adopted the anti-Catholic

position, ammunition for the maintenance of which lay close
to his hand. Instead, he assails the position.

The remarkable thing about William Penn is that when
he spoke of religious toleration he really meant what he said.
There was no tinge of hypocrisy in him. He did not decide
in advance to rule out a particular creed, and then marshal
his logic in such a way as to come out at the proper conclusion
while making grandiose talk about believing in universal
freedom. He would not have had *anyone* penalized for following his conscience, except when a perverted conscience led
to crime or vice (the kind of limitation that he thought any
sane man has to accept). When he defended freedom of
religion, he meant equality before the law and the government.

By the reign of James II, Penn had ceased to speak in the
fashion of Milton about the abominations of Rome: his
Seasonable Caveat against Popery was fifteen years behind
him, and he was no longer the heated anti-Catholic propa-
gandist he had been. With a Catholic on the throne, it would
have been undiplomatic, and moreover his friendship with
James Stuart could only have convinced him that Catholics
were not necessarily diabolical. Perhaps James had persuaded
him of the falsity of one idea of which Locke would make
much, namely that Catholics were under no compulsion to
keep faith with heretics.

During James' reign Penn wrote three major works on the
subject of religious toleration. *A Persuasive to Moderation to
Church Dissenters, in Prudence and Conscience: Humbly
Submitted to the King and His Great Council* (1686) was an
appeal for an end to the Test Act, drawn up mainly with
the Dissenters in mind, but also advocating sufferance for
everybody, including Catholics. *Good Advice to the Church
of England, Roman Catholick, and Protestant Dissenter*
(1687) appeared after the Declaration of Indulgence, defend-

ing the King's action, and appealing for Parliamentry approval. *The Great and Popular Objection against the Repeal of the Penal Laws and Tests* (1688) was a direct reply to Halifax's *Letter to a Dissenter*.

In these writings the author went down the list of accusations against the Church of Rome, treating the subject so systematically and comprehensively as to give the reader a very good summary of how anti-Catholic Englishmen felt.

Penn denied the customary accusation that no Catholic government can ever be anything but a persecutor with other religions. He noted numerous instances to the contrary in European history. His stock example was Cardinal Richelieu, who broke the political power of the Protestants but allowed them to worship freely in their own bailiwicks. As early as 1670 Penn had mentioned "the timely Indulgence of Henry the Fourth and the discreet Toleration of Richelieu and Mazarin." Penn had heard much of the Richelieu-Mazarin administration of France while he was at Saumur, for his professor and host, Moses Amyraut, was a Huguenot who had known both Cardinals and had been consulted by both about Huguenot affairs. Amyraut was not the only non-Catholic to be favored by the Princes of the Roman Church. There was the more noteworthy case of Turenne, Mazarin's military commander. "It was an Huguenot then, at the Head of almost an Huguenot Army, that fell in with a Cardinal himself (see the Union, Interest makes) to maintain the Imperial Crown of France, and that on a Roman Catholicks Head : And together with their own Indulgence, that Religion, as National too, against the pretences of a Roman Catholick Army, headed by a Prince brave and learned of the same Religion."

That passage was pertinent, given the current behavior of France under the leadership of Louis XIV. More remarkable is Penn's readiness to point out that the Anglican argument about Catholic persecution in England was by no means the last word. In one passage he even suggested something approaching an extenuation of the Marian persecution :

I know it is said, The Blood-shed in the fore-going Raign, and the Plots of the Papists against Queen Elizabeth, drew those Laws from the Church of England. But this was no reason why she should do ill because they had done so. Besides, it may be answered, that that Religion having so long intermixt itself with worldly Power, It gave way to take the revenges of it. And certainly the great men of the Church of England endeavouring to intercept Queen Mary, by proclaiming Lady Jane Gray, and the apprehension the Papists had of the better Title of Mary Queen of Scots, together with a long Possession, were scurvy temptations to kindle ill designes against that extraordinary Queen.

Penn was not asserting anything so fantastic as that Mary Tudor was justified in her treatment of heretics. He was criticizing the Church of England, the persecutor in power, and so put the brief for the other side as convincingly as possible. He *did* impugn the Anglican argument about the political need for the penal laws. That was his rationale.

Penn always held for a close bearing of politics on the religious denominations. He took up one of the main talking-points of his adversaries, the Revocation of the Edict of Nantes, and boldly attributed this measure less to the Catholicism of Louis XIV than to his royal tyranny. Penn suggested that the King of France would not retain the Revocation longer than he believed it in the interest of his personal rule : "But let us see the end of this Conduct; it will require more time to approve the Experiment." Penn had good reason to speak thus : he knew that Louis XIV had quarreled with and insulted the Pope when it suited him, and was not regarded as a paladin of Catholicism by his Catholic neighbors.

The conclusion to which Penn came after pursuing the

logic of his argument to the limit was this: "Violence and Tyranny are no natural Consequences of Popery, for then they would follow everywhere, and in all places and times alike."

For Penn, religion and politics should always be viewed as interacting when penal laws in favor of one particular creed are under discussion; and the candor of an autocrat should always beheld suspect when he appeals to his religion as the excuse for oppressive measures. To this extent there is no distinction between Catholics and Protestants, all being men and therefore subject to the same human weakness for domination. Both alike must reject tyranny of any kind, once they understand their religion; both may or may not became enemies to liberty, depending on the politics amid which they live. Consequently it is impossible to justify England's penal laws on the ground that a resurgence of the Catholic Church would mean a return to Mary Tudor or an imitation of Louis XIV. The way to obviate the danger is to prepare the political stage in such a way as to prevent any ecclesiastical actors from hogging it. Make governmental tyranny impossible, and you make religious tyranny impossible. If you must remember Mary Tudor, you ought not to forget Henry VIII and Oliver Cromwell.

Penn sounded very pro-Catholic, and indeed the good faith in which he defended the Catholics of his period is beyond reproach. *His* villain of the piece was not the Church of Rome but the Church of England, for he was attempting to reason out a satisfactory solution to the existing dilemmas, and his first problem was to break the dictatorial power of the Anglicans. After that he would have had the Dissenters and the Catholics brought into partnership with the Anglicans under the common name of Englishman. He would have had a condition of "Our Superiours governing themselves upon a

Ballance, as near as may be, towards the several Religious Interests."

Not that he would have decried the privileged place of the Church of England. His idea was to allow it a superiority based on its numbers, and to allow a proportionally smaller power to smaller groups unable to accept the theology of the establishment. He thought this would have been accomplished if only Charles II's Declaration of Indulgence had been accepted in Parliament as the law of the land: "Then it was that we looked like the Members of one Family, and Children of one Parent. Nor did we envy our eldest Brother, Episcopacy, his Inheritance, so that we had but a Child's Portion."

Despite his defense of the Catholics, Penn was no more pro-Catholic than pro-Anglican or pro-Dissenter. He denounced those in power and backed those out of power, but was by no means hopeful of seeing them change places. He wished that ecclesiastical domination as such would disappear. In the context of English politics that could only come about by a curtailment of the authority of the Church of England, which is the end toward which he worked.

During the reign of James II the soundness of Penn's logic came under fire since it was maintained by nervous Protestants that they could not be at ease as long as a Catholic sat on the throne. To dispel this fear, if it could be dispelled, was one of the tasks to which Penn devoted himself.

The King's Sincerity

When James II first met with his Privy Council following the death of Charles II, he made a brief declaration of his intentions. With regard to the religious question he remarked: "I know the principles of the Church of England are for monarchy and the members of it have shewed themselves good and loyal subjects, therefore I shall always take care to defend and support it."

His words were greeted by the Anglicans with relief and gratitude; yet three years later they helped to push the King from his throne. That short space of time saw a progressive disillusionment on both sides, beginning with the first promptings of doubt, moving through annoyance, resentment, and declared hostility, and ending in victory for one side and catastrophe for the other. The King had misjudged the Anglicans from the start. They had misjudged him.

When James contemplated the sacramental character of the High Church theology, when he saw the apparatus of bishops and altars and surplices and censers, he could not doubt that here was something very like his own Catholic religion. All that was needed was obedience to the Pope. He entertained high hopes that many an Anglican ecclesiastic would go over to Rome now that the King was a Catholic. His feeling reinforced his desire to remove the disabilities on his Catholic subjects. He expected to succeed even with recalcitrant Anglicans because of their expressed policy of nonresistance to the Crown.

While James II was reasoning thus, the bishops of the Church of England were interpreting his thoughts quite differently. They took his pledge to them to mean that he would make no effort to bring either them or their dioceses around to his creed. They expected him to maintain their establishment in all of its existing privileges as well as its rights, so that while the King might privately worship in a manner offensive to them, at least he would do nothing to upset Anglican supremacy in his kingdom. Above all, they set forth as *the* criterion of his rule that he should not tamper with the Church of England for the benefit of the Church of Rome.

The exaggerated Catholicism that James proceeded to

display had, in consequence of this mutual misunderstanding, the opposite result from the one he intended. Anglicans in general did not become less, but more, anti-Catholic. They showed themselves increasingly obstinate under such goadings as Magdalen College, the activities of the newly-erected Court of High Commission, the appointment of Catholics to positions formerly reserved to Anglicans, the trial of the Seven Bishops.

James, for his part, would not have been so demanding had the Church of England carried on as he presumed it would. In his words and acts it is possible to discern a disappointed man, baffled and incensed by those in whom he had put so much trust. The provocation was strong on both sides. It was a vicious circle of injuries recoiling upon themselves : the Anglicans opposed the King because he appointed Catholics to office; the King ostentatiously made such appointments because of the Anglican opposition. They accused him of breaking his word; he accused them of disloyalty.

James might have been less forward except that he had another group of non-Catholics on which to rely. Rebuffed by the Anglicans, he turned to the Dissenters. It is not true that he conveniently discovered the latter in order to exploit them; William Penn's whole career at Court states the contrary, and we know that James had not despaired of Anglican compliance when he ordered the Quakers released from prison; but having found the Anglicans unyielding about their dominant position, he had to go elsewhere, and so to the Dissenters he went when he decided to get rid of the penal laws and the Test Act.

James was not even then bent on doing real harm to the Church of England. He did indeed commit unwise and illegal acts when supplanting Anglicans with Catholics; but some of these he doubtless would have defended as simple restitution, while others he might have confessed were mistakes provoked by exasperation. At any rate, he himself never admitted that he had broken his word to the Anglicans.

They accused him of dishonesty when he promulgated the Declaration of Indulgence, although he had taken pains to forestall the charge by insisting on what he considered to be Anglican rights as covered by his pronouncements. The Declaration "repeated the king's promise to maintain the established church, and declared that he had no intention of disturbing the holders of monastic and church lands secularized in the Tudor times." But that was not good enough for the men he was trying to mollify.

It was good enough for William Penn, who would not agree that under James the Church of England had been harmed in violation of the royal oath.

> To object the King's promise, when he came to the Crown, against the repeal of the Penal Laws, shows not his Insincerity, but her Uncharitableness, or that really she has a very weak place : For it is plain the King first declared his own Religion, and then promised to maintain hers ; but was that to be without, or together with his own ? His Words show he intended that his own should Live, tho t'other might Raign. I say again, it is not credible that a Prince of any Sincerity can refuse a being to his own Religion, when he continues another in its well being.

The attitude of James and Penn comes down to the same thing. Both would preserve the rights of the Church of England; both would preserve certain of its privileges but not others; both would eradicate its power to oppress non-Anglicans. That was *their* definition of the word "maintain." But the bishops of the establishment had formulated a different definition.

Penn put the blame squarely on the bishops : "And if the Church of England will but be advised to give him the opportunity of keeping his repeated Word with her, and not deprive her self of that advantage by Jealousies and Distances

that make her suspected and may force him into another
Conduct, I cannot help believing that the King will not to a
tittle let her feel the assurance and benefit of his Promises."

The Church of England was to blame; the King was right
about the Catholic question; the Dissenters ought to have
followed the King. Addressing the Dissenters, Penn exhorted
them: "Be not Couzn'd, nor Captious, at this Juncture. I
know some of you are told, if you lose this Liberty, you introduce Idolatry, and for Conscience sake you cannot do it. But
that's a pure mistake, and improv'd I fear, by those that know
it is so, which makes it the worse; for it is not Introducing
Idolatry (taking for granted that Popery is so) but saving the
People from being Destroy'd that profess that Religion."

Penn's warning to the Dissenters not to be taken in by
the Anglicans is a fact worth remarking since a famous
polemicist on the other side, the Earl of Halifax, was warning
them not to be taken in by the King. Halifax, able politician
and articulate penman, took it upon himself to keep the
Protestants of England aware of the Catholic menace. He
stood to the anti-James forces as did Penn to the Court, and
so it is not surprising that ultimately they collided in a personal duel. Halifax's *Letter to a Dissenter* (1687) is well
known. Penn's rejoinder ought to be better known: *The
Great and Popular Objection against the Repeal of the Penal
Laws and Tests* (1688).

Halifax began the personal innuendoes while urging the
Dissenters not to accept the Declaration of Indulgence at the
hands of the King. Noting the Quakers' happy reception
of the measure, he added the jibe: "I should not wonder,
though a man of that Perswasion, in spite of his Hat, should
be a Master of Ceremonies." In reply Penn scoffed at "their
Master-piece, the *Letter to a Dissenter*," and took issue with
Halifax on almost every clause of his anti-James indictment.

Halifax said that his pamphlet had two points to make:

"The first is, the cause you have to suspect new Friends. The second, the Duty incumbent upon you, in Christianity and Prudence, not to hazard the publick Safety, neither by desire of Ease, nor of Revenge."

This meant in the first place that the Dissenters should not trust the King: "Consider that not withstanding the smooth Language which is now put on to engage you, these new Friends did not make you their Choice, but their Refuge: They have ever made their first Courtships to the Church of England, and when they were rejected there, they made their Application to you in the second place."

Penn did not deny that James' first hope was to establish religious toleration through a rapproachment of the Anglicans and the Catholics. What Penn did deny is that the King ever had in mind an Anglican-Catholic alliance to persecute the Dissenters: it was a political maneuver to throw the preponderant strength of the kingdom behind freedom of conscience for all. The fact that he had to go to the Dissenters as an alternative, Penn did not set down to his discredit: the fault lay with the Anglicans and nobody else. As for the King's integrity: "It is a Misfortune to be lamented, the Church of England should always be against Liberty, when the Court is for it, because the Court, in her opinion, is not Sincere. . ." That the King *was* sincere is proved rather than disproved by his desire for the Declaration of Indulgence: "That which moves him to it, must oblige him to maintain it; and if he does not heartily intend to support this liberty, his giving it, must needs increase the Power and Interest he would suppress: An Error too gross to be made with so much Preparation and Art."

Halifax held it a manifest contradiction to believe that a Catholic monarch can in good faith promote religious toleration: "This Alliance, between Liberty and Infallibility, is bringing together the Two most contrary things that are in the World. The Church of Rome doth not only dislike the allowing Liberty, but by its Principles it cannot do it. Wine is not more expressly forbidden to the Mahometans, than giving Hereticks Liberty is to Papists."

Penn denied the major premise and argued that infallibility and liberty can theoretically cohere side-by-side. The contradiction that shocked *him* was that in which the Church of England was caught. Speaking of the Dissenters who thanked the King for the Declaration of Indulgence, he asserted: "So that tho it is true that they joyn with the Papists, it is as true that it is not with Popery but for Liberty, which the same Author tells us, is such a contradiction to Infallibility, which is his dangerous Popery: Tho I must tell him, I think it a greater to Persecute People upon a professed fallible Principle."

If Catholic faith is not inconsistent with religious freedom, do Catholic governments in fact ever tolerate Protestantism? Penn had an affirmative answer ready to meet Halifax's negative. The Earl wrote of the Catholics that "they allow no Living to a Protestant under them. Let the Scene lie in what part of the World it will, the Argument will come home, and sure it will afford sufficient ground to suspect."

The implication in the remark touched in particular the Revocation of the Edict of Nantes. Penn, who had met and rejected this argument before, regarded Halifax as putting forward a fallacy either from ignorance or from dishonesty.

We look on France till we frighten our selves from the best means of our worldly Happiness, but will not look at home upon greater Cruelties, if we consider theirs [the Catholics'] were exercised against those of another Religion, but ours upon the People of our own [Protestantism]; tho when we observe their Conduct elsewhere, it is easie to see, it must have something very particular in it. But at the same time we will take no notice of the greatest Tranquility in Germany and Switzerland under a compleat Liberty.

Halifax would have had the Dissenters trust the Church of England because of a change that had come over her leaders. He used a double standard. Having condemned the King for conciliating the Dissenters only after failing to wheedle anything from the Anglicans ("these new Friends did not make you their Choice, but their Refuge," etc.), Halifax blandly put the Anglicans in the right for switching from the King to the Dissenters.

If you had now to do with those Rigid Prelates, who made it a matter of Conscience to give you the least Indulgence, but kept you at an uncharitable distance, and even to your more reasonable Scruples continued stiff and inexorable, the Argument might be fairer on your side ; but since the Common Danger hath so laid open that Mistake, that all the former Haughtiness towards you is for ever extinguished, and that it hath turned the Spirit of Persecution, into a Spirit of Peace, Charity, and Condescention ; shall this happy Change only affect the Church of England ?

Penn would have had the Dissenters be very wary with the Church of England until they saw some signs that the leopard had changed her spots : "If she affects an Union, why should she uphold the means of Division? Ought not the Dissenters to Suspect her Integrity, in refusing a good Understanding, in the very way that must save those she would gain? . . . She can't think we ought to trust her, That won't Trust, and that makes Trusting Dangerous." Again : "If she will please but to tell me what way she can secure the Dissenters against her own Ambition, when one of her Communion Ascends the Throne, I will undertake to tell her, how she and the Dissenters may be safe from the Danger of Popery in the Reign of a King of that Religion."

Halifax looked to a partial religious freedom, one to in-

clude the Dissenters but carefully excluding the Catholics :
"Are you so linked with your new Friends, as to reject any
Indulgence a Parliament shall offer you, if it shall not be so
Comprehensive as to include the Papists in it ?"

Penn looked to a universal religious freedom, one to include
both Dissenters and Catholics—which is to say that he
favored the Declaration of Indulgence as promulgated by
James II. He thought the arguments against the King were
absolutely ludicrous, and he struck at the heart of Halifax's
case with this passage : "But that we should be less safe
because the King, [whom] we so Fear, is ready to Consent to
a Great Charter for Liberty of Conscience, by which it shall
be Declared the Right of Mankind to make a free and open
choice and profession of Faith and Worship towards God,
and that any Constraint or Interruption upon that Freedom
is Impiety and Evil in it self. . . . is, I must confess, a Notion
very Extraordinary."

The Halifax-Penn duel sums up like this. Halifax urged
Parliament to maintain the Test Act, Penn urged the legis-
lature to throw it out; Halifax doubted the honesty of the
King, Penn defended it; Halifax suspected the Church of
Rome, Penn the Church of England; Halifax warned the
Dissenters not to be deceived, and so did Penn, but with
opposite deceivers in mind.

In the practical outcome Halifax won the duel. His *Letter
to a Dissenter* was read. Penn's *Great and Popular Objection
against the Repeal of the Penal Laws and Tests* was not read.
James II's Declaration of Indulgence went by the board with
his fall, and the Catholics were not relieved of their civil
disabilities until the nineteenth century.

That Penn's reasoning was the poorer of the two is not so
evident. Sir Winston Churchill has pronounced the *Letter
to a Dissenter* "cogent"—but without validating it against
Penn's logic. Or Penn's history. Or Penn's prophecy. Penn

was afraid of Anglican domination of the religious life of England, and that was just what England got with the Toleration Act of 1689. The Dissenters were not enfranchised : they became second class citizens along with the Catholics. They learned just how much truth there was in Halifax's saying that the Church of England's "former Haughtiness towards you is for ever extinguished." They saw little enough of that "Spirit of Peace, Charity, and Condescention" of which he had spoken so glibly. Daniel Defoe, author of *The Shortest Way with the Dissenters* (1702), could have had some pertinent information for the author of *A Letter to a Dissenter*.

To Penn's defense of James there is a standing objection— the King's reaction to the Revocation of the Edict of Nantes. According to Turner, Louis XIV's persecution of the Huguenots drew from the King of England "wholehearted enthusiasm." The basis for the assertion is what James told Barillon. Yet Turner explicitly notes the obvious truth that James was not the soul of candor in speaking with the envoy from France, and even gives a quotation that represents James as saying that "he abhorred the employment of 'booted missionaries' in France as impolitic and unchristian." This declaration James made to the ambassadors of Spain and Holland. To hold that he was dishonest with them and honest with the French ambassador is simply gratuitous, and all the more since James had powerful political and financial reasons for placating Versailles. Moreover, the Anglican Bishop of Bath and Wells commented on "His Majesty's royal goodness" in asking alms for the Huguenot refugees in England.

James understood and deprecated the unfortunate effect of the Revocation on his own government. The Earl of Abingdon, protesting against any repeat of the penal laws, "told his Majesty he would find great difficulties in this matter, because that he knew his neighbor on the other side of the water had broke through all laws and promises, so that no-body knew what to trust. The King said he knew that, but could not tell how to help it. As for his own opinion, it had always been otherwise."

To assert that James applauded the attempt to convert the Huguenots is one thing; to assert that he approved of Louis' methods is quite another. He advised his son, the Old Pretender, never to try to make converts to Catholicism by force. There is no proof that he was hypocritical about this. Let it be added that he was an exile in France, a pensioner of Louis XIV, when he made the statement.

As the crisis of the reign grew more ugly, Penn, striving to ward off attacks on the King's probity, wrote an appreciation of James II that he alone of all Englishmen was capable of writing.

> Whatever Practices of Roman Catholicks we might reason-ably object against (and no Doubt but such there are), yet he has disclaimed and reprehended those ill Things by his declared Opinion against Persecution, by the Ease in which he actually indulges all Dissenters, and by the Confirmation he offers in Parliament for the Security of the Protestant Religion and Liberty of Conscience. And in his Honour, as well as my own Defence, I am obliged in Conscience to say that he has ever declared to me, *It was his Opinion.* And on all Occasions, when Duke, he never refused me the repeated Proofs of it, as often as I had any poor Sufferers for Conscience-sake to solicit His Help for.

There is the key to Penn's feeling about James II. He had known James more than casually for fifteen years. In 1673 James, as Duke of York, told Penn he advocated religious toleration short of a breach of the peace. After 1685 James, as King, repeated the same sentiment on many occasions, and released crowds of Dissenters from their prison cells. His Declaration of Indulgence simply extended the sentiment,

codified it, and made of it a principle of practical politics.
Penn judged it out of the question, even apart from everything else, that such consistency could spring from fundamental insincerity.

Penn was speaking from his personal experience, which
fully validated, in his opinion, the self-defense that James
inserted into the Declaration of Indulgence :

> We cannot but heartily wish, as it will easily be believed,
> that all the people of our dominions were members of the
> Catholic Church. Yet we humbly thank Almighty God
> it is, and hath of long time been, our Constant sense and
> opinion (which upon divers occasions we have declared)
> that conscience ought not to be constrained, nor people
> forced in matters of mere religion ; it has ever been directly
> contrary to our inclination, as we think it is to the interest
> of the government, which it destroys by spoiling trade,
> depopulating countries and discouraging strangers ; and
> finally, that it never obtained the end for which it was
> employed.

The King's Power

Penn had satisfied himself that James II was not engaged
in a Machiavellian scheme in which, unless checked, he would
entice the Dissenters to his side, wangle them into helping him
raise up the Catholics, and then punish both Dissenters and
Anglicans with Romanist intolerance. The Quaker courtier,
censor, and eulogist of the reign did not leave it at that : he
never depended on mere good will at the palace, least of all
when controverting those who doubted its existence. To the
argument from the King's sincerity he added an argument
from the King's power — and he regarded the latter as con-
clusive, whatever may have been said of the former.

Halifax had told the Dissenters they were crazy to think
of letting their fate be decided by the mere word of a Papist

monarch : "Your former Faults hang like Chains still about you; you are let loose only upon Bayl; the first Act of Non-compliance, sendeth you to Jayl again." Penn's answer was that no such trust is either necessary or implied, for there are strong practical motives to keep the King and the Catholics true to their pledge :

And tho it is Imagin'd the Dissenter has no other bottom for his Confidence and Conjunction then the Roman Catholicks Faith and Truth, 'tis too mean an Insinuation against his understanding . . . . Nothing, humanely speaking, fixes any Man like his Interest ; And tho this Agreement were only Hobson's choice in Roman Catholick and Dissenter, the security is not the less : For if I am sure of them by the side of Interest and Necessity, I will never seek or value Ensurance by Oaths and Tests.

"Interest" was a defining term in Penn's practical and political philosophy. He used it in various senses, depending on the context and on the books he had in mind. Sometimes it carried the technical meaning attached to it by classical theorists like Machiavelli and, more especially, John Harrington, author of *Oceana,* one of Penn's favorite sources. Sometimes it had connotations in Penn that seem to anticipate the superficial cynicism of the eighteenth century.

What he meant by it when discoursing of politics was generally this : the behavior of men should be anticipated or explained by their estimation of what they stand to gain or lose in money, power, influence, fame, security, at any turn of the circumstances. Granted that true belief and right conduct are taught by a higher authority than egoism (conscience or the Inner Light), yet when non-moral, and of course immoral, conduct is under examination, then "interest" is the essential factor. Isolate this psychological spring of action, and you can be fairly certain how men are going to behave — in daily life, in society, in politics, in ecclesiastical affairs. It is a happy conjuncture when conscience and profit go hand-in-hand, as when Richelieu and Mazarin tolerated the Huguenots. It is a deadly misfortune when they become separated, as when Louis XIV refused to tolerate the Huguenots; and then the ideal is to fuse them again, for "interest" is too powerful to be left unguided by moral considerations. From this trend of thought came Penn's prediction that Louis would bring back the Edict of Nantes, his pious posturing notwithstanding, the moment he thought it to be for the advantage of his royal absolutism.

Referring to the Declaration of Indulgence, the word "interest" meant that the Catholics had nothing to gain from hypocrisy. Short of universal toleration they would live in perpetual danger, their numbers being too insignificant to gain them any predominance. Oddly, Halifax had placed in Penn's hand a weapon with which to strike at the *Letter to a Dissenter*. Starting a trend that would be followed by Whig historians for centuries afterward, Halifax minimized the percentage of English Catholics in the nation: "Let us be still, quiet, and undivided, firm at the same time to our Religion, our Loyalty, and our Laws, and so long as we continue this method, it is next to impossible, the odds of two hundred to one should lose the Bett."

Two hundred to one. Was it conceivable that in the face of such numbers a royal plot really could bring about Catholic ascendancy in England? Penn thought not. "In my opinion 'tis Groundless; for since their Master-piece, the *Letter to a Dissenter* tells us, that there can be no danger of the Bet, where the Odds are so great as Two Hundred to One, we must conclude that Objection is of no weight against our Liberty: For Number being the Natural Power of a Kingdom, the Artificial (which is the Executive part of a Government) must needs move heavily and dangerously when it works against it."

The dilemma into which Penn pushed Halifax was one

that clutched at the Whig interpretation when it accused James extravagantly of engineering a Romanist conspiracy against the Protestants, and at the same time denied that his co-religionists amounted to more than a tiny minority contemned by the overwhelming majority of the English people. Penn realized that one horn of the dilemma must, in mere good sense, be abandoned : either no such conspiracy, or else a greater number of Catholics to make it believable. Compared with Penn, Halifax seems more naive than cynical, and so do a host of Whig historians who have soberly set down the contradiction as historical truth. In our own time James' biographer has assured us that under this King England was "a nation fanatically and incurably hostile to the Roman faith." Just why the fury of the big majority should be visited on the small minority by means of the Test Act — this remains as unclear as when Penn was duelling with Halifax.

The same dilemma applies to the fear of conversions to Catholicism that might occur should the anti-Catholic laws be repealed. The Whig historians who believe this a well-grounded fear, and who fasten on the conversion of Dryden as a hint of what might have happened to many other Englishmen, should logically drop one clause of their creed: either no danger of England returning to the old faith, or else England much less opposed to that faith than is suggested by the anti-James propaganda. Penn dropped the first clause : "What they convert upon the Square, Persuasion I mean, is their own and much good may it do them. But the fear is not of this; and for compelling the adverse Genius of the Kingdom, they have not the means, whatever they would do if they had them." It is arguable that he adopted the wrong alternative. It is certain that *one* alternative *had* to be adopted to the exclusion of the other.

Penn understood that there were Catholics who, of all Englishmen, would be the last to accept his diagnosis of their

situation—those like Petre who dreamed of regaining the
predominance their ancestors had enjoyed and who really
believed they could reverse the historical trend could they but
seize the levers of power. For their own good, as well as for
that of the rest of the nation, Penn implored them to open
their eyes to the hard reality—their political impotence before
the united opposition of an irrevocably Protestant England :
"I say then this Unity, this Universality and this Visibility
against Popery, makes the attempt for *more* than Liberty of
Conscience too great and Dangerous. I believe there may be
some poor silly Biggots that hope bigger, and talk further, but
who can help that? There are weak People of all sides, and
they will be making a Pudder."

But so much is not the whole story. This minority was not
even at one with itself. The Catholics of England could not
agree about what was best for them, and it is even possible
that most of them disliked the King's policy because of the
way it angered their non-Catholic neighbors. James received
numerous warnings from Catholic sources at home and
abroad, including one from the Pope, who was afraid that
the gains from the period of physical persecution would be
lost by pressing for too much too soon. Petre by no means
represented the prevailing opinion. Penn made prominent
use of

the Intestine Division among themselves. That Division,
weakens a great Body, and renders a small one harmless,
all will agree. Now that there is such a thing as Division
among them is town talk. The Seculars and Regulars have
ever been two Interests all the Roman Church over, and
they are not only so here, but the Regulars differ among
themselves. There is not a Coffee-House in Town that
does not freely tell us that the Jesuites and Benedictines
are at variance, that Count [d'Adda] the Popes Nuncio and
Bishop Lyborn Dissent mightily from the Politicks of the

first ; Nay t'other Day the Story was that they had pre-
vail'd Entirely over them. The Lords and Gentlemen of
their Communion have as warmly contested about the
lengths they ought to go. Moderation seems to be the
conclusion. Together they are little, and can do little ;
and divided, they are Contemptible instead of Terrible.

Penn's point about the internal disputes of English Catholics is supported by Trevelyan, who speaks of "the handful
of half-unwilling Roman Catholics whom [James] was thrust-
ing into a perilous supremacy." This historian insists that
James had to have help from outside his Communion and
that he therefore approached first the Anglicans and then the
Dissenters; but it is still maintained that James threatened to
force Catholicism on England — although how this could be
effected through the "half-unwilling" never emerges during
the discussion. Penn had noted the problem in 1687. His
solution was to see James striving, not for Catholic ascendancy, but for universal toleration embracing Catholics,
Dissenters and Anglicans. Penn's solution was not patently
inferior to Trevelyan's.

Halifax condemned the Declaration of Indulgence as an
assault on English law and warned the Dissenters that
"the Law is so Sacred, that no Trespass against it is to be
Defended. . . . After giving Thanks for the breach of one
law, you lose the Right of Complaining of the breach of all
the rest."

Penn's reaction to this thought may easily be inferred. The
King was not asking for no law; he was asking Parliament to
replace one law with another, and an unjust law with a just
one. He was not demanding that the nation accept his royal
fiat; he was appealing for legislative concurrence. Penn felt
as strongly as Halifax that the law is sacred. It is precisely
for that reason that he impugned Halifax's thesis as an absurd
piece of sophistry. Penn formulated his idea of what England

needed in these words: "If we can but once see a Magna Charta for Liberty of Conscience, Established in these Kingdoms by the wisdom of Parliament, They will be very Hardy indeed, who Dare, at any time, Attempt to Shake It, That has the Jealousie, Union and Resolution of so many Great, Serious and Wealthy Interests to support it."

To the most fearful Protestants Penn said in effect: Suppose King James to be a monstrous liar cloaking fierce intolerance with a pretense of believing in universal toleration — what then? The reply he conceived to be apparent as soon as the religious, social, and political lines of force were examined. He was categorical that the King had not the power to do what his enemies said he would unless he were stopped now. He could not Catholicize England. Penn's conception of the existing situation linked up with his political theory, where (following James Harrington) he held that the kind of government a state has depends on how the land is parceled out. Since the landed gentry controlled England and spoke through Parliament, it followed that the religion of the gentry could not be destroyed overnight — the motives and purposes of the King being for this reason almost irrelevant. A Catholic coup d'etat was impossible.

His reasoning allowed Penn to consider without qualms the hypothesis of James II being a furious and intolerant Romanist. He was willing to accept, for the sake of argument, the picture of the King pressing for full Catholic domination of England, for Penn foresaw an outcome that must be entirely different — namely, freedom for every religion, or at least for the three great divisions of Anglican, Dissenter and Catholic. A royal fight for an impossible Catholic *domination* could, he thought, if it made any headway at all, produce nothing more than Catholic *toleration*; and this in turn involved toleration for every creed since only under the umbrella of universal freedom would the rest of the nation, the immensely greater part, consent. Presume, Penn argued, presume James Stuart as infernal as you like; you cannot, nonetheless, compromise the plain truth that he would never be able to Catholicize England.

Penn discovered himself thinking along lines parallel to those of the King. Penn wanted freedom of conscience for everybody in order to achieve freedom of conscience for Quakers. James wanted freedom of conscience for everybody in order to achieve freedom of conscience for Catholics. To the cynics who alleged this as the King's purpose, Penn would have retorted — Of course, and a good thing too.

7
PENN, JAMES
AND ENGLISH LIBERTIES

The conspirators who made the Glorious Revolution of 1688 had a second major complaint against James II. They considered him a tyrant as well as a bigot. To their suspicion of his religious policy they added the suspicion that he planned to rule as an absolute monarch and without Parliament, as Louis XIV ruled without the States-General of France. They thought that English liberties were no less endangered than the Church of England by the King's use of the royal prerogative to by-pass Parliamentary enactments. More, they alleged that James was a traitor to his own crown and that at the opportune moment he would ask Louis for help, whereupon a French army would be transported across the Channel to crush English patriots and permit the King of England to rule his realm as a viceroy of the King of France. Again, did James intend to offer his realm as a fief to the Holy See? The bare query was an effective weapon in the arsenal of his enemies.

They were sure that they knew his strategy. They watched him closely to find out his tactics in every set of circumstances, and they promptly labeled as a tactical maneuver everything he did. If he acted despotically (for example, with Magdalen College), he was only acting according to his true nature. Should he behave in what looked like a constitutional manner (for example, when he asked Parliament to approve the Declaration of Indulgence), then the sly hypocrite was coming out in him. They developed their own criteria and applied them in such a way as to arrive always at the judgment they had decided in advance *must* be the right one.

Between this blunt opposition to practically everything in the reign and the Petre-Sunderland support for practically everything, there lay the inevitable middle ground. Here stood those who believed that James II was fundamentally sound but capable of egregious misapprehensions and undoubted illegalities. Here stood William Penn.

Penn denied the postulate of his adversaries by insisting on the correctness of James' attitude toward English liberties. That he should do so followed logically from his defense of James' religious policy, for religion and politics interacted. If the King's prerogative might legitimately be used in behalf of the Declaration of Indulgence, then it would have been a self-contradiction to hold that the dispensing and suspending powers were as such illegal. Having declared the King justified on the religious issue, Penn naturally found him justified on the political issue.

Penn was not working up an argument ad hoc in holding for James' constitutionality. He was not entering unfamiliar territory because his chosen path took him into it. For almost two decades he had been writing (and preaching) about English history, law, institutions, government. He had participated in politics, had entered elections to defend the type of candidate who would uphold his concept of the rights of Parliament. He brought to his estimation of James II a mature and systematic theory of what English liberties were and how they might best be ensured.

Penn's Theory of the State

He began at the beginning, with communal life in general. A full-blown abstract political philosophy in the manner of

Hobbes and Locke is not to be expected of him. He was too earth-bound, too empirical, for that. As he had no more theology than was necessary to what he thought ethical behavior should be, just so he had no more ideology than was necessary to what he thought political behavior should be. His characteristic pragmatism saved him from the morass of political mythology no less than from the mysic absurdities of sectarianism.

The sources on which he drew for his theory of the state cannot be pinpointed. The major influences, however, whether they affected him directly or indirectly, can be guessed with a reasonable degree of certitude. Penn's aspirations are from Plato and St. Augustine, his theory of man as a social being is from Aristotle, his political morality is from Grotius, his conception of English rights is from Coke, his governmental machinery is from Harrington. Behind them all towers the Bible, preeminently the majestic figure of St. Paul. Anyone who bears these seminal sources in mind can easily make sense of Penn's attitude to English liberties.

He saw everything conditioned by the natural law, which enjoins the Golden Rule on the individual and justice on the state. Justice is the reason for one man's holding power over another : "By Government we understand an external Order of Justice, or the right and prudent Disciplining of any Society by just Laws, whether in the Relaxation or Execution of them." Justice means giving every man his due. Justice in government means sharing rights and duties equitably among the population; and this leads directly into deciding cases at law, inflicting punishment, and the whole apparatus by which an administration contributes to the healthy functioning of the body politic. A large part of government is, obviously, non-moral (the rule of the road, etc.). Penn knew about such cases from reading, from common sense and observation, from his work as legislator for Pennsylvania. He did not dis-

parage this part of politics. But his principal concern was
political morality in the strict sense, for the violation of this
produced not merely physical disorder but vice and even
crime. He wanted to teach the state how to make men do
what they ought to do, and what they would do if they
obeyed the precepts of the natural law. Men left to themselves
are disobedient, a moral infirmity descending from the primal
disobedience of Adam and Eve.

> When the great and wise God had made the world, of all
> of his creatures it pleased him to choose man his deputy
> to rule it; and to fit him for so great a charge and trust,
> he did not only qualify him with skill and power, but with
> integrity to use them justly. This native goodness was
> equally his honour and his happiness ; and whilst he stood
> here, all went well ; there was no need of coercive or com-
> pulsive means ; the precept of divine love and truth in his
> own bosom was the guide and keeper of his innocency.
> But lust prevailing against duty, made a lamentable breach
> upon it ; and the law, that before had no power over him,
> took place upon him and his disobedient posterity, that
> such as would not live conformably to the holy law within
> should fall under the reproof and correction of the just
> law without, in a judicial administration.

Our first parents, expelled from the Garden of Eden,
entered the world of toil and sin. Man was on his way to the
making of the state. By what process did this actually come
about? Penn had available to him two prime solutions to the
question. Aristotle's patriarchical theory told him that society
began with the authority of the father, and that the state arose
through the amalgamation of families into clans, of clans into
villages, and of villages into city states. The alternative was
the social contract theory, most familiar to Penn's generation
in the version of Thomas Hobbes, who wrote that men
existed first as isolated self-sufficient units, and then came
together through a compact agreed upon by all of the indi-

viduals involved. Hobbes used the theory to argue for absolutism in government, holding that by the social contract the people handed over all authority to their sovereign. Later John Locke made a libertarian theory of it by resurrecting the analysis of Althusius and Pufendorf, by adding to the *social* contract which formed society a *governmental* contract between society and the government, the latter being limited by the terms of the contract. The theory of the contract was used by the revolutionaries of 1688 to defend their conspiracy against James II.

Penn's opinion of the supposed primitive compact was ambiguous. He spoke of it differently in different contexts. He was favorable to it when arguing for a European union in his *Essay Towards the Present and Future Peace of Europe* (1693). Since the basic problem here was to gain consent from the various governments, he aproached close to the idea that organized life began with a contract. Asserting the nations of his time to be in "that sovereign or independent state of men that was previous to the obligations of Society," he went on to add that the crowned heads have the same interest in an international arrangement that individual men had when they first consented to live in society—namely security and order. Society itself being the result of "a reasonable design in men of peace," surely a similar "reasonable design" might now put an end to war and the pretensions of the nations against one another? It was part of Penn's pragmatic approach to politics to insist on the plausibility of the social contract theory when he was trying to get an international contract signed.

Elsewhere he took a different view of it. With Aristotle he saw that to live in groups, at least as far as the family, is natural to man. He quoted the key Biblical texts that speak of the fate of Adam's children and their posterity. He reasoned that, the bond of charity broken, men had to have some other principle by which to deal with one another, and this could only have been the authority of the father: "Government is an expedient against confusion; a restraint upon all disorder; just weights and an even balance: that one man may not injure another nor himself by intemperance. This was at first without controversy patrimonial, and upon the death of the father or head of the family, the eldest son or male of kin succeeded."

So much of a starting point was sufficient for Penn. He had found his premise, and he felt no compulsion to go further. He might have outlined a fully Aristotelian theory, which he was too cautious to do because he did not feel confident about his theorizing when he came to the post-patriachal epoch. Government at that time, he said, "is as hard to trace to its original as are the copies we have of the first writings of sacred or civil matters." He would not go all the way with Aristotle, but neither would he mythologize about the social contract as did Hobbes before him, Locke in his own time, and Rousseau after him.

Penn's inconsistencies about the origin of society are due to more than his unwillingness to go beyond the evidence, to more than his pragmatic desire to limit himself to shoring up practical political guarantees. He did not follow Aristotle to the end, as he might have been expected to do, because he was looking for a sharply-etched theory of consent. Admitting that the source of patriarchical authority was the natural law, he could not suppress the conviction that government must in some sense involve the free will of the individual—consent being "natural" too—and he was unable to work out a complete system that would make room for both. He could not bridge the gap between the non-voluntary subjection of children to their parents and the voluntary subjection of citizens to their government.

In any case he was Aristotelian enough to take society as

he found it. His real concern was with government, the unifying principle of society, not with the primitive historical process that produced them. It was enough for him that both are demanded by human nature itself, the full progression (logical, not necessarily temporal) being: society — justice — law — magistracy — government. No less than Aristotle would he conclude: "Hence it is evident that the state is a creation of nature, and that man is by nature a political animal."

Government is thus from nature. It is also from God. The judgment of Aristotle is vindicated from a higher source, the Pauline texts: "Render unto Caesar the things that are Caesar's," "The powers that be are ordained of God," etc. St. Paul laid it down that government is the result of pride and transgression. So did William Penn, who gave as the upshot: "This settles the divine right of government beyond exception, and that for two ends; first, to terrify evildoers; secondly, to cherish those that do well; which gives government a life beyond corruption and makes it as durable in the world as good men shall be. So that government seems to me a part of religion itself, a thing sacred in its institution and end."

Government has a divine right in both senses of the phrase. It is instituted by God; and its function is to assist man to the achievement of beatitude in the next world. The bare existence of the Inner Light is not enough to save all individuals, many of whom must be pressured or otherwise guided into the kind of conduct that will save them. The magistrates who exert such pressure, far from hurting the natural law, are helping along the divine plan for the salvation of humanity.

But if there is a divine right of government, what about the divine right of kings, so beloved of James I? For William Penn there was no such thing. He had learned from Aristotle that at least three legitimate systems are possible, although he may have taken this particular lesson more immediately from Moses Amyraut, who puts it to his readers that "there are three kinds of simple government, the popular, the aristocratic and the royal, in each of which power is as absolutely sovereign as it is in either of the others."

Following this line of reasoning Penn argued that the idea of a "best" form of government is absurd, for while consent is part of every good system, that consent may be to anyone of the three alternatives, or to any combination of them. It all depends on the historical experience of any given people, so that if the French want absolute monarchy, the English constitutional monarchy, and the Swiss democracy, then it is proper for these three different systems to exist in Europe at the same time. A review of past history makes the thing even clearer since a multitude of governmental ideas have been tried and found to be successful.

To turn the argument to the other side, there is one infallible mark of a bad government, and that is tyranny. Wherever freedom is destroyed, and above all the freedom of the governed to save their souls as their consciences direct them, the ruler has no moral claim to his authority. It is an inversion of the purpose of government, which is justice, so that unjust government is under the natural law a contradiction in terms. Tyranny exists, unhappily, but only as long as it holds the sword: "Government has many shapes, but it is sovereignty though not freedom in all of them."

If force pertains to legitimate rule, whether monarchical, aristocratic, or democratic, it is only within the bounds of the moral law, when of course it may and should be used without apology by the authorities. "If any should ask me: What are the things properly belonging to Caesar? I answer in Scripture Language: To love Justice, do Judgment, relieve the Oppressed, right the Fatherless, and in general be a Terror unto Evil-doers, and a Praise to them that do well: for this is the end of Magistracy. And in these things they are to be obeyed of Conscience as well as Interest."

Obedience is a duty of the governed, authority is a right of the government, in any society that is correctly oriented toward the ultimate good of man. Not that secular power can save a man's soul, or should even try; that is up to him individually under the guidance of his Inner Light; but it can provide him with the freedom to follow his Inner Light and dissuade him from obnoxious acts, and it can extinguish evil and corrupting influences in the rest of the body politic. It thereby does his work and its own at the same time, for thieves, murderers, adulterers, vagabonds, gamblers, "are the Evil-goers that violate those laws which are necessary to the Preservation of Civil Society."

Government is therefore universal, while the form of government is relative to time, place, and public sentiment. The practical measure of what is right here and now is prescription—the right of existing institutions to remain just because they happen to be already there. Penn would have been the last to say that no room should be left for improvement, but he accepted the sensible argument that the easiest way to achieve political ends is a rule-of-thumb approach to what is already in existence. If this should become tyrannical or otherwise intolerable, he would counsel passive resistance, the kind he practised when he broke the law but offered no violence to the police who dragged him off to court or to jail.

The function of government is to make laws, execute them, and see that those who break them are punished. In any society there must be laws of two kinds: "Laws Fundamental which are Indispensable and Immutable; and Laws Superficial, which are Temporary and Alterable." Natural law becomes human law when interpreted by "Right Reason," the working of the human mind in such a way as correctly to infer the bidding of nature. Positive law should be reasonable too, in the sense of not being irrational, but the legislator need not go to nature for it; in fact, nature probably will not give him what he want if he does, for there are usually alternatives equally permissible.

Penn mentioned most of the obvious attributes of law — that it must be promulgated so that the people will know what is expected of them, that it must be enforced, that it must be obeyed by magistrates as well as the public, that breaches should be punished promptly, that punishment should not exceed the offense.

When he turned to the question of how to secure good government and sensible obedience in the governed, he became Platonic. Like Plato he found that education is basic; denying that good institutions are the foundation of a good polity, he alloted that place to good men, without whom he thought institutions no matter how sound to begin with are sure to be destroyed from within.

Penn had had experience of the religious training of children, and he thought political training should supplement it. He stood for the education of the young to be future citizens. He admired the schools of the Jesuits for their administration and curriculum, for their combination of the humanities and sciences, a not uncommon reaction even among Protestants. The Jesuit institutions were the admiration of Europe. Penn would take over the system developed by the sons of St. Ignatius, but ordered to a more Protestant purpose: "Let us use Methods not inferiour to theirs, but for better Ends. Let us employ our Skill to improve the Children's Natural Abilities, to excite them to Virtue, and endear the True Interest of their own Country to them."

Penn's ideal was a state submitting to the universal law of God and nature; governed by a constitution peculiar to itself since created by historical causes, social experience, and good sense operating within actual conditions; manned by a virtuous and patriotic citizenry fulfilling their duties, demanding their rights, and facing the future with confidence in the moral integrity of the rising generation. He would have agreed that, men being sinners, the ideal could never be found in operation. He certainly was made aware of the truth by his Pennsylvanians, who distressed him immensely by becoming increasingly restive under his direction. But Pennsylvania was an afterthought. His political theory he formulated in the first instance as a commentary on events taking place in his native land.

The English Constitution

The proper government for England is one made up of King, Lords and Commons. Penn accepted the form as readily as did any Englishman of his time, more intelligently than most since he judged his country's constitution by theory as well as by vague patriotic instinct. He knew about the historical dialectic of King versus Parliament and had lived in the period when dispute had given way to war. His own decision, when he grew old enough to think about it, was to side entirely with neither, partially with both. His advocacy of James II makes him seem too much of a Royalist, but that is an illusion comparable to his role of exaggerated pro-Catholic. His apology for the King, like his apology for the Catholics, took its character from the circumstances of the moment. His earlier labors in behalf of Algernon Sidney had indicated that his constitutional philosophy was far wider than crude Royalism. His writings make it possible to see all the facets of that philosophy.

Putting aside the question of a natural law supreme over all human authorities, considering positive law as independent and properly coercive within its legitimate limits, Penn went to the past to find the reasons why England should be ruled

according to a particular system. He would not commit the
genetic fallacy and set up historical development against
morality, but morality being safeguarded, he held that past
history is a valid criterion. If he was not an historian, he had
read the historians far enough to make use of them for his
own purposes; he could, when he found it necessary or
desirable, invoke Coke's notion of the immemorial common
law of England, or Harrington's theory that English freedom
came out of the German forests with the war bands that overthrew Roman Britain. Historical theses such as these were
being vigorously debated throughout the century, and Penn
was abreast of them.

When he defended the dispensing power of the Crown, the
right of the King to override laws made in Parliament, this
was no plea for arbitrary rule since he took the dispensing
power to be part of the old English constitution as well as
something that ought to exist under the natural law. To
prove the correctness of his interpretation he suggested to his
opponents: "Let us compare our Civil Transactions with the
Ancient Laws and Statutes of the Realm: This is English."
When he does this, he finds not the King but Parliament to be
the disrupter of the primeval system: the legislation aimed at
producing religious uniformity "seems to be an Alteration in
the ancient English Government, by making Ecclesiastical
Conformity the Grand and Necessary Qualification in Englishmen to the Peaceable Enjoyment of their Natural and
Civil Inheritance."

The Angles and Saxons, he said—following a dubious turn
of thought that began with Tacitus and his noble Teutons—
brought with them to England a rude form of democracy in
which key rights were fundamental: life, liberty, property,
voting of laws, participation in the administration of justice.
Penn accepted all of these as part of the legal, political, and
social inheritance of Englishmen. Like Coke he was credulous

about the antiquity of English rights contained in the common law. Like Coke he relied on unreliable historians who appealed to him — notably Andrew Horn, who traced the common law back to the Saxons and King Alfred, and William Lambarde, who tried to underprop the theory by denying that the Norman Conquest brought any real change. From these Penn took the thesis that the primeval Teutonic system survived unblemished into the Middle Ages, where he found it entrenched in historic documents like Magna Carta. The Great Charter is a constant theme of his. He thought so much of it that he caused to be printed its first American edition (1687), and he considered it to be a central bastion of English rights.

> I know it is usually objected that a great Part of the Charter is spent on the Behalf of the Roman Church, and other Things now abolished ; and if one Part of the great Charter may be repealed or invalidated, why not the Other ? To which I answer : That renders nothing that is Fundamental in the Charter the less valuable ; for they do not stand upon the Legs of that Act, though it was made in Honour of them, but the Ancient and Primitive Institution of the Kingdom.

Magna Carta was a principal reason for Penn's willingness to see some good in political Catholicism. Protesting the enforcement of the penal laws he wrote : "Further let it be weighed that we come not to our Liberties and Properties by the Protestant Religion; their Date rises higher." He was speaking here of legal guarantees for certain individual rights. He knew that heresy was not protected in the Middle Ages, and he was happy to see that part of the medieval legacy abandoned; but he argued that the Reformation proved hardly less intolerant, especially in England : "The Parliaments of England, since the Reformation, giving no Quarter to Roman Catholics, have forced them to the Crown for

Shelter. . . . On the other hand, the Crown having treated the
Protestant Dissenters with the severity of the Laws that
affected them. . . . they have been driven successively to the
Parliaments for Succour."

Penn's argument from England's recent past seems dis-
cernible in the Declaration of Indulgence when James II says
of religious equality : "And in this we are the more confirmed
by the reflections we have made upon the conduct of the last
four reigns; for after the frequent and pressing endeavours
that were used in each of them to reduce the kingdom to an
exact conformity in religion it is visible the success has not
answered the design, and that the difficulty is invincible."

Penn took the liberties originating in Germany and codified in the Middle Ages to be gravely jeopardized by post-
Reformation England. At the same time he found a post-
Reformation oracle to query about these liberties, namely Sir
Edward Coke, who had championed the rule of common law
in defiance of James I and his divine right of kings. Apparently it was Coke's writings more than anything else that
taught Penn how to quote appropriate legal texts with
dispatch and to the point. Penn knew the law and the legists
(Lincoln's Inn fortified by subsequent reading). He had
polished his ability to use both, as came out in the Penn-Mead
trial (of which he published the proceedings) when he first
called for a hearing according to the common law and then
protested against the illegal behavior of his judges.

> Certainly, if the Common Law be so hard to be understood,
> it's far from being very Common ; but if the Lord Coke in
> his *Institutes* be of any consideration, he tells us that
> Common Law is Common Right, and that Common Right
> is the Great Charter Privileges : Confirmed 9 Hen. 3. 29. ;
> 25 Edw. 1. 1.; 2 Edw. 3. 8.; Coke Inst. 2. p. 56.
> I appeal to the Jury, who are my Judges, and this great
> Assembly, whether the proceedings of the Court are not

the most arbitrary, and void of all Law, in offering to give
the Jury their Charge in the absence of the Prisoners. I say
it is directly opposite to, and destructive of, the undoubted
right of every English prisoner, as Coke in the 2 *Inst.*, 29.
on the Chap. of Magna Carta speaks.

If so able a manipulation of technical law seems remarkable in a non-professional, it is only typical of William Penn.
He meditated at length about the legal implications of free
citizenship. He then went out into the highway to defend
those implications. His history is not above suspicion; he
tended to idealize the past because he unconsciously made it
closer to his ideal than it was; but his legal thought was
remarkably sound and, better than historic, prescient. To his
credit is the public example he set. Brought into court, he
could bandy words with the best of his prosecutors: he
sought to make them look ridiculous, and not only when legal
technicalities were under discussion. At the start of the Penn-
Mead trial he threw his accusers back on the defensive after
a brief skirmish. They were trying to catch him out on the
Quaker refusal of hat honor:

Mayor. Sirrah, who bid you put off their Hats. Put on
their Hats again.
Whereupon one of the Officers, putting the Prisoners' Hats
upon their heads (pursuant to the Order of the Court)
brought them to the bar.
Recorder. Do you know where you are?
Penn. Yes.
Recorder. Do you know it is the King's Court?
Penn. I know it to be a Court, and I suppose it to be
the King's Court.
Recorder. Do you not know there is respect due to the
Court?
Penn. Yes.
Recorder. Why do you not pay it then?

Penn. I do so.

Recorder. Why do you not put off your Hat then ?

Penn. Because I do not believe that to be any respect.

Recorder. Well, the Court sets forty Marks apiece upon your Heads as a fine for your contempt of the Court.

Penn. I desire it might be observed that we came into the Court with our Hats off (that is, taken off) and if they have been put on since, it was by order from the Bench ; and therefore not we but the Bench should be fined.

On several other occasions as the trial progressed Penn got the better of a duel with words. Thus :

Recorder. "Sir, you are a troublesome Fellow, and it is not for the honour of the Court to suffer you to go on."

Penn. "I have asked but one Question, and you have not answered me, though the Rights and Privileges of every Englishman be concerned in it."

Recorder. "If I should suffer you to ask Questions till to-morrow morning, you would never be the wiser."

Penn. "That is according as the Answers are."

No wonder the trial was punctuated with cries from the bench of "Take him away, take him away!" and "Pull that fellow down, pull him down!"

Penn was not simply trying to be impudent or unconciliatory on principle. It was all part of his deadly serious counterattack against assaults on the fundamental rights of Englishmen as he interpreted them. At the Penn-Mead trial the right in jeopardy was the freedom of juries to bring in verdicts without being browbeaten by judges; Penn's conduct throughout was intended to stiffen the resolution of the jury in the face of a hostile bench; and he won, for the jury defied the judges and repeatedly, doggedly, brought in the verdict that finally stood up — "Not guilty." This is known in English law as "Bushel's case" from the name of the foreman of the jury and being vindicated by a later court ruling helped establish an integral part of subsequent courtroom procedure. It is the perfect example of how William Penn fought successfully for a right he took to be guaranteed by the traditional constitution of England.

One other right must be mentioned — the right of property. For Penn it was as important as any other: "The first and most fixt Part of English Government." Here he was speaking rather of English positive law than of the natural law; plainly he would not have placed property before individual liberty or freedom of conscience. All Quakers were sensitive about the fruits of industry, for they lay under the perpetual threat of confiscation, a crippling penalty for people who were mainly debarred from making a living in any other way. More than that, property is customarily considered basic by political philosophers, and Penn agreed with them in theory just as he agreed with the Friends in practice. His ultimate judgment was that "Where Liberty and Property are violated there must always be a State of Force." Every man has a right to independent action and to the rewards of his labor, a right founded in the natural law and guaranteed by English law.

The trouble in England, as he saw it, was that too many men of authority were assiduously violating both. Theoretically he found England superior to France because "In England the Law is both the measure and bound of every Subject's duty and allegiance." But in practice there was little to choose between them. That was why he felt so pessimistic about the future of his country, for he could not believe that divine judgment would be long delayed in the case of a people so given to persecution, of a magistracy so little concerned for the maintenance of rights or the suppression of vice. That was why, among his hopes for the future, not the least significant turned on the very existence of the Friends, the Children of Light, the one group really prepared to seek for the will of God and to do it. With the Old Testament in mind he exhorted the Quakers to stand apart from the rest of mankind in their morals and manner of life, for to them was given a transcendent mission : "We are the People above all others that must stand in the Gap and Pray for the putting away of the Wrath, so that as this Land be not made an Utter Desolation."

His religious standpoint is critical to his politics. But he never lapsed into a mysticism that would allow no appeal except to the theological. He threw himself into the campaign for hard legal guarantees, pressing for an England that might admit the communal law of justice as an institutional fact even if charity itself were unobtainable. His support of James II's Declaration of Indulgence was given for the purpose of restoring the historic system by which religion was divorced from politics — a system that he himself constructed to a certain extent from his creative imagination, but also grounded firmly enough in historical fact to bear some resemblance to reality. Even if his picture of medieval institutions was idealized, still the great cogs in the machinery of government — King, Parliament, Common Law, Magna Carta — did come down from the Middle Ages. Hence his boast that "above all Kingdoms under Heaven it is England's Felicity to have her Constitution so impartially Just and Free." He wanted to keep it that way.

The King's Sincerity

Penn's theories of the state and of the English constitution are essential to an interpretation of his apology for James II. They prove that he was no ignoramus getting out of his depth when he summoned to James' aid both the abstract corollaries of the natural law and the historic intricacies of the common law. His personal involvement strengthens his position. As early as 1670 he was agitating for his legal rights.

As late as 1682 he was establishing a new political entity dedicated to those rights and many more. In between, the year 1678 saw him out in the hustings in search of traditional constitutional rights, defending an independent Parliament against the Crown. As he stood beside his King, therefore, he did so with an awareness as total as his commitment.

There is no hope of arguing that Penn helped James to violate English liberties because he did not know what those liberties were. There is no hope of charging that royalty either dazzled or cowed him into acquiescence. His reaction to Magdalen College and the Seven Bishops is a flat disproof; so is the courage with which he defended, even under examination by William of Orange, his friendship with the fallen Stuart sovereign. Penn believed that James wanted to preserve rather than to harm the constitution of the realm. Penn believed that James was as sincere about English liberties as about religious toleration.

When James II met his Privy Council after the death of Charles II, he gave his pledge to maintain the Church of England and termed himself equally favorable to the rights of Englishmen. "I have been reported a man for arbitrary power; but that is not the only story which has been made of me. I shall make it my endeavour to preserve this government both in church and state, as it is now by law established. . . . I have often heretofore ventured my life in defence of this nation, and I shall go as far as any man in preserving it in all its just rights and liberties."

These words, too, the King's enemies called hypocritical, charging that as he harmed the Church of England while supposedly protecting it, just so he tried to whittle away the political freedom he had promised to support.

Penn took the negative side in the debate. He did not mention all of the allegations, but usually it is possible to infer his opinion from his broad principles. Take the Court of High Commission : was it not illegal, and so an indication that James II did not faithfully accept the rule of law? Penn had two answers open to him on the basis of his systematic thought. He might have confessed it was technically illegal but denied it to be an attack on the just claims of the Church of England; or, more characteristically, he might have taken it to be a necessary contravention of a bad positive law for the sake of the natural law of justice — the right of the King to be a Catholic, and as such to turn his Anglican duties over to Anglicans. Penn's absolute preference, which he knew to be impossible, was for the Church of England to be disestablished altogether.

But James exerted pressure on his judges to get a decision favorable to the dispensing power! Yes, said Penn by implication, and that was precisely the proper thing to do to judges who would put laws passed in Parliament above the laws laid down by nature itself. This was no proof that the King wanted to drop the law overboard and rule by arbitrary decree. It meant that he subordinated the lower law to the higher, as he should have.

James' continuation of the customs dues before Parliamentary approval, his desire for the recall, or at least emendation, of the Habeas Corpus Act — these were not things Penn felt called upon to judge as right or wrong. Less enthusiastic adherents of the King than he admitted, with regard to the first, that James had merely taken, in the words of a twentieth century historian, "the technically illegal but perfectly reasonable step of ordering the collectors of customs to carry on their duties as before." As for habeas corpus, Penn could not have been opposed to the law itself, but might have accepted its restriction in certain cases where the Crown was involved. That he hoped to see the power of indefinite arrest restored is not to be seriously considered; and he was not worried about the possibility that James was bent on restoring that kind of power.

The Whig indictment was and is that James II broke the law. Penn, who fully understood that the question of law was only a blind for an essentially religious move, could have and should have laughed sardonically at the spectacle the Whigs provided when they had got rid of James. The thing looks like a satire, almost a Gilbertian burlesque. Parliament denied the throne to James II and gave it to William III; but only the King of England could summon Parliament; hence England was without either King or Parliament, and legally must remain so. According to Maitland the fundamental contradiction was this:

Grant that parliament may depose a king, James was not deposed by parliament; grant that parliament may elect a king, William and Mary were not elected by parliament. If when the convention met it was no parliament, its own act could not turn it into a parliament. The act which declares it to be a parliament depends for its validity on the assent of William and Mary. The validity of that assent depends on their being king and queen; but how do they come to be king and queen? Indeed this statute very forcibly brings out the difficulty—an incurable defect.

The "incurable defect" did not prevent the members assembled from seeking a legal basis for the change of sovereigns. Perhaps it should be held that James II had abdicated? But that would mean a regency, with the throne to be held for his son, a Catholic. Perhaps James should be declared insane? The same answer. Must it then be said that James was still King of England? No—they would not pursue the legal argument that far.

In the end they invoked the theory of a governmental contract, declared that James had violated the agreement between him and his subjects, and concluded that his subjects had simply exercised their right to depose him. English law was not permitted to interfere with so satisfactory a consummation. One Whig historian applauds the decision because "common sense was destined to triumph over sentiment and an exaggerated respect for technicalities."

The epilogue is almost too exquisite in its ironic commentary. The Tories who refused to accept William III became Jacobites or Jacobite-sympathizers. The Anglican clergymen who took the position that they could not swear an oath of allegiance to William without breaking the one they had already sworn to James, became Non-Jurors; they abandoned their livings rather than conform against their consciences and began a dissident tradition within Anglicanism that did not die out until the nineteenth century. Among the original Non-Jurors were *no less than five of the Seven Bishops.*

Penn, himself under fire because of his friendship with James, could not very well give the public his analysis of the new order in England — even though the manner in which it came into being vindicated to a startling degree his before-the-fact testimony that the legal darts hurled at James came from men who were not especially devoted to either the law or the constitution.

Penn had never believed that James was maneuvering to destroy English liberties. The King overtly presumed the legislative rights of Parliament in everything he did, and Penn accepted him at his face value. To Penn it appeared fantastic that anyone should accuse the King of plotting to close Parliament as the States-General were closed in France; for the French popular assembly had never been open since Richelieu's time, while the House of Commons and the House of Lords were viable, energetic, even headstrong, political institutions that had revealed their power when they confronted Charles I, that had thrust back Charles II when his policies became irritating to them, that were fighting with James II. James might prorogue one Parliament or dissolve it; he might strive to pack the Commons, throw his influence into its sessions, and denounce the members furiously when they voted against him; but that he even dreamed of closing the doors for good was beyond Penn's imagination.

James had never hinted at such a thing. His expressed conviction that kings are accountable only to God has often been quoted to the detriment of his reputation. What has not so often been quoted is the advice he gave to his son as a guide should he recover the throne: "Apply your self principally to know the Constitution of the English Government, that you may keep, both you and your Parliament, each in due Bounds that become the one and the other."

Was it the interested liberalism of a broken tyrant? The Earl of Abingdon could not have thought so, for at the climax of the reign he had a long interview with James in which both men implicitly assumed the rights of Parliament in the government of the kingdom. It was when the King asked Abingdon to help persuade the counties to send members to Parliament who would vote for the Declaration of Indulgence.

> He said it may be I was for another judgment myself, and so had no mind to do it, and therefore he desired to know what my opinion was. Whereupon I told his Majesty, since he was pleased to ask my opinion, I hoped he would not be angry at my declaring it, and would do it very plainly and freely. Upon which his Majesty replying he would not, I told him, I should not make any preface nor put him off to the meeting of a Parliament; that if there was a Parliament now sitting, as my opinion now was, I should be against those things, but I was not so settled in that opinion or prejudiced, but if I did see reason, or were convinced upon the debate, I might alter it. His majesty said my answer was like my character etc. and that I had done with him like a man of honour and worth etc.

To several other men James said much the same thing. If he cherished illusions about the attainable, a coming overthrow of Parliament was assuredly not one of them.

Penn was persuaded of James' soundness in domestic affairs. His sentiments were the same about the King and his foreign policy, specifically the relations with France. The accusation was rife that the King of England hoped one day to play the puppet to Louis XIV. James gave his own retort when he said angrily to the Dutch ambassador: "Vassal! Vassal of France! Sir, if Parliament had wished, and still wished, to give me the necessary means, I would have carried the monarchy, and would still be carrying it, to a prominence as great as it ever enjoyed under any of the kings my predecessors. . . ."

The words "necessary means" identify a central problem of the reign. Charles II had found it necessary to go to Louis XIV for funds because Parliament would not vote him what he needed to rule England. James inherited the same dilemma. It does not follow from his accepting French gold that he did the bidding of the French monarch. An odd feature of the liaison was that James and Louis were suspicious of one another. Louis' suspicion showed through when he ordered Barillon to tighten the purse-strings until James should dissolve Parliament and be obliged to use force against his subjects; and the French envoy in London "represents James as extremely out of humour with France on this account, and that he talked of holding the ballance of power in his hands." James began to pursue an independent foreign policy, most defiantly with William of Orange, Louis' *bete noire* and the man who eventually would seize James' throne. So did the kaleidoscope shift.

We cannot tell how much Penn knew about the subtleties of the Stuart-Bourbon relationship. Silence is never a good argument with him, given his confidential status at Whitehall, and he must have heard about the gold that went from Versailles to London, something that would not have shocked him since receiving money from a foreign government did not bear in the seventeenth century the stigma it would have today. Penn must have known of James' reluctance to place his reliance on Louis, and of Louis' distrust of James.

As for James Stuart as an Englishman, Penn never doubted his patriotism. He had had personal experience of the Lord High Admiral under fire during the Dutch War, and had heard more about his service with the Navy from Sir William Penn. The idea that a man of this character would jettison his old feelings on mounting the throne seemed ridiculous to Penn, who had noticed not the merest intimation of it. And patriotism apart, Penn could not believe that so strong-willed a personality, so proud a sovereign as James II, would bend before a rival monarch or demean himself so far as to accept his crown from an alien hand.

There is a poignant story about James' patriotism dating from the moment of ultimate defeat. He watched the naval Battle of La Hogue (1692) when the French were repulsed in their bid to open the Channel for his return home. James Stuart, former King of England, saw his hopes dashed beyond recall. James Stuart, former Lord High Admiral of the English navy, remarked that only his English sailors could win such a victory.

The King's Power

Having argued from psychology, from James' intentions, Penn, in his customary fashion, turned for a look at empirical reality, at the existing facts within the framework of which James must act. The argument about English liberties balances on the same fulcrum as the argument about religious toleration. For a second time Penn's logic was that the King's sincerity was immaterial because of his capabilities (or *in-*capabilities). Assuming James II to aim at tyrannizing over his kingdom, Penn was forced to conclude, not that there was any real danger of royal despotism, but that the King was suffering from delusions.

At the beginning of the reign Penn drew certain inferences about James that were falsified by time. He held the King's age, fifty-one, to be an obstacle to his free pursuit of insidious objectives like intolerance; but James lived to be sixty-seven. Penn held the want of a Catholic male heir to be insurance against any attempt on entrenched Protestantism, for whatever James did might be undone immediately after his death by his Protestant daughters; then James' Queen ruined this syllogism by giving birth to a son. Although they lapsed eventually, these were not simply talking points for use in a debate. James' enemies felt their force and hoped to see the problem of a Catholic monarch solved speedily and without violence. James was moved by the same notion, which accounts for a lot of his rashness : he believed, for example, that unless he himself did something for the Catholics, and quickly, nothing ever would be done for them. Penn was familiar with the King's motives and did not condemn them. His pro-James pamphlets, in any case, did not stand or fall with the King's age and heirs. These were minor items, the disappearance of which left the major ones unaffected.

What Penn said about politics is similar to what he had already said about religion. In his estimation the bulwarks that shielded England from tyranny were much the same as those shielding the nation from intolerance. This was true to an eminent degree of the traditional constitution of the realm as Penn interpreted it — Magna Carta, separation of creed and citizenship, King and Parliament independent of one another, with neither dominant, and both respecting the natural law and the common law. Similarly, the danger to the constitution, to English liberties, was identical with the danger to religious toleration.

James II was being accused of creating just such a danger. Penn spoke to the contrary. Unequivocally, almost harshly, he singled out Parliament as the disturber of the peace. His fear was that the legislature, reflecting the overriding might of Whigs and Anglicans, of aristocrats, squires, magnates and wealthy merchants, would become a multi-headed despot for want of any adversary capable of standing up to it. He perceived the warning signs in the passing of the Test Act, ostensibly a religious measure, but by its character effectively intervening in the non-religious life of England, disfranchising countless men and women who had no redress until the King came to their assistance with his Declaration of Indulgence. Should Parliament win this battle, Penn foresaw Whig tyranny matching Anglican intolerance. He could not anticipate the subsequent development of Parliamentary omnipotence, but implicitly he condemned it in advance. The old "divine right of kings," the future assertion that "Parliament can do anything" — these notions are equally contradictions of his theory of the English constitution. King *and* Parliament — he cannot reason properly in politics without both.

Where the opposition took the power of the Crown, as wielded by James II, to be a menace to freedom in England, Penn took it to be a guarantee of that freedom. He held the optimum condition to be one in which the strongest individual in the realm (the King) represented the weakest faction (the Catholics), and the weakest individuals (the members of Parliament) represented the strongest faction (the Anglicans). Let both sides work as hard as they can for their own interests, each necessarily trying to attract as many Dissenters as possible, and there is a good chance of stability resulting in liberty for the nation.

Such being Penn's idea, it seems odd that he failed to press it home at one crucial interview. James II commissioned him to sound out William of Orange at The Hague, and to see whether William, married to the heiress to the English throne, would join with him in an expressed hostility to the Test Act. The conversation followed this pattern, according to Bishop Burnet: "Pen said the king would have all or nothing: but that, if this were once done, the king would secure the toleration by a solemn and unalterable law. To this the late repeal of the edict of Nantes, that was declared perpetual and irrevocable, furnished an answer that admitted of no reply."

But of course it *did* admit of a reply, and we can only wonder why Penn did not give it (*if* he did not: Burnet is too antagonistic to Penn to be above suspicion as a reporter of this interview). Louis XIV was a Catholic ruler of a predominantly Catholic nation, and moreover an absolute monarch who never had to deal with an independent legislature, or indeed any legislature at all. *He* could persecute France's Huguenot minority with impunity. James II enjoyed no such royal supremacy. Unlike the Sun King, James was a Catholic ruler of a predominantly Protestant nation, and a limited monarch confronted by a legislature not only independent but hostile. Louis tore up the Edict of Nantes of his own free will, his personal whim. An English enactment of the same character could not be withdrawn except by sovereign and legislature acting together. James was unable even to extort Parliamentary concurrence with his suspension to the Test Act, something much less excessive than the Revocation of the Edict of Nantes. Therefore the guarantee offered to William by Penn was no paper promise, but rather a true law founded on an equilibrium of two political institutions already expressing themselves through workable governmental machinery.

William's reference to the Revocation, delivered with so much self-assurance if we can believe Burnet, was preposterously wide of the mark. Why did Penn not indicate the fallacy? Perhaps he was caught off-guard by the sophism, perhaps he had not yet perfected his thought on the subject, for the interview at The Hague took place before the crisis in England became acute and forced him to work out a thoroughly reasoned approach to English politics of the moment.

William's answer hardened Penn in his Stuart loyalty for the same reason that it drew Burnet more tightly to the side of the great adversary of the reigning King of England. For Penn, there could be no real freedom as long as any Englishmen were penalized politically for their faith. For Burnet, the Catholics were a standing menace to be coerced for the good of the nation. The Penn-Burnet antithesis at The Hague is a paradigm of subsequent disputes in and out of Parliament, so that if you understand the animosity between these two men you can more easily follow the turns and twists of English politics for two centuries afterward.

Penn returned to London disillusioned about the possibility that William would put an end to Anglican dominance of the religious life of England. His report to James was a decisive factor. The King saw that if oppression was to be lifted from his co-religionists, it could have to be his own work : he could no longer count on a non-Catholic to do it for him. The result was the Declaration of Indulgence. Its failure did not give Penn any reason to re-examine his belief that the King could not take away the power of Parliament, while Parliament was in fact undermining the power of the Crown.

The Whig historians commonly retort that James II had an army, the one he kept up to strength after Monmouth's defeat, and which he insisted on staffing with Catholic officers despite the Test Act. Camped on Hounslow Heath near London, these forces caused a lot of apprehensive comment. The fact is, however, that the morale of the troops testifies to the correctness of Penn's insight, and one prominent Whig historian can be compelled willy-nilly to be a witness for Penn. Trevelyan says that the Londoners hated the camp on Hounslow Heath, "rightly regarding it as a menace to their liberties and their religion." He calls James "a military despot." He then roundly vindicates the Protestantism of the vast majority of the men under arms and ascribes to them "a profound belief that papists deserved to be hanged scarcely less than rebels." The army, on Trevelyan's showing, was a broken reed in James' hand—as we might expect since the nation itself was no more reliable: "nine-tenths of [James'] subjects were in opposition to his will." Trevelyan, to put comment in the mildest possible form, does nothing to invalidate Penn's argument that James could not come close to being "a military despot."

But Louis XIV had an army, the very reliable troops of a Catholic tyrant! Was the French army not a dagger poised to strike England at a signal from James? Was not the Revocation of the Edict of Nantes scheduled to have its companion piece in England with the aid of French bayonets? Those who replied affirmatively noted a speech by the Bishop of Valence. John Evelyn recorded in his diary that the Bishop thanked Louis XIV for the Revocation and said "that God seem'd to raise the French King to this power and maganimous action, that he might be in capacity to assist the doing of the same here [in England]." Englishmen of Evelyn's cast of mind did not invariably put so much faith in the sermonizing of a French ecclesiastic.

Penn had no faith in the Bishop of Valence. He knew the last thing James wanted to see was a French invading force: "But certainly we must be very silly to think the King should suffer so great a shake to his own Interest as admitting an

Army of Forraigners to enter his Kingdom on any Pretence must necessarily occasion."

Supposing, nonetheless, the worst of James II, supposing him to be waiting for the great day of French intervention in his behalf—what then? Penn's first response was that any troop convoy sailing from the coast of France would be sunk by the Royal Navy. This may be a compound of bravado and patriotism, an appeal to both elements in his English readers. His real point was that Louis XIV could not send enough soldiers across the water to conquer a stubbornly Protestant nation, and of course had no intention of making the attempt while he was facing formidable enemies on the Continent, while a lesser force would have to depend on a Catholic rising inside England, with too few Catholics to carry out the assignment.

Nor could James do more than pray for a coalition of Catholic states to lend him arms and men. In hard fact, and James knew this as well as Penn or anyone else, no coalition was possible. There were too many conflicting international interests to permit it. The current European whirligig had Louis XIV poised against the King of Spain, the Holy Roman Emperor—and the Pope. (The latter two Catholic powers would soon be united with Protestant England to curb the pretensions of Catholic France). This being so, at least two specific anti-James accusations were inconsistent: he could not have intended both to make England a puppet of France *and* to offer his kingdom as a fief to the Holy See. The historical fact is that the "vassal of France" intrigued against France in his foreign policy, and the "vassal of the Pope" refused to listen to the Pope about the religious affairs of his realm.

Penn's moral was that James II could not subvert freedom in either religion or politics, even if he wished to do so—which he did not.

The sceptics refused to be persuaded. The leaders who sent the invitation to William of Orange were doubtless divided among themselves about how many articles of their indictment reflected reality and how many were being alleged merely for propaganda purposes; they were not divided about the desirability of having another king on the throne. Penn was swamped. James himself proved to be of no help. If he would not be cautious in his own interests, how might his suspicious subjects be expected to be moderate in theirs? Barren of aplomb, unyielding when he should have been conciliatory, jealous of his royal station, he could not and would not compromise with good grace. Many English Catholics realized he was ruining the cause he desired to save; they knew that the Sunderland-Petre clique, by reinforcing the impliable side of the King's character, were threatening them with another round of abuse, and just when it seemed that they had survived the worst and might now live in peace as a powerless minority. However much they might applaud James' policy in the abstract, they could not contemplate with equanimity the likeliest practical consequences. But even the Pope could not get a hearing at Whitehall when he urged James not to promote Catholicism so rashly.

Penn has indicated what went wrong with the reign of James II. One of his most perspicacious apothegms about politics is the following: "Let the people think they govern and they will be governed." James, by his undiplomatic actions, turned the saying to the other side: "Let the people think they do not govern, and they will not be governed." Despotism may have been (as Penn argued) beyond his grasp; he may not (as Penn argued) have grasped for it; but he provoked in too many Englishmen the dread that he was about to snatch away their freedom and persecute their religion. That was why he lost his throne.

8

THE GLORIOUS REVOLUTION

JAMES' REIGN ended in chaos. By the time he yielded and offered the indispensable concessions—summoning Parliament (despite his failure to pack it), abolishing the Court of High Commission, allowing the Fellows of Magdalen to return to their college—by this time it was too late. William of Orange landed in England and marched on London, joined along the way by most of James' military commanders led by John Churchill, later Duke of Marlborough. As the tide turned with irrevocable momentum, the anti-James magnates declared for the Dutch invader.

James II, abandoned by Louis XIV, whose help he had rejected, unnerved by treason, fearful that his father's fate might be his if he lingered too long, had his son carried over to France and then took flight himself. Everything he did redounded to William's advantage. His refusal to stay and fight disgusted the army. The removal of the heir to the throne simplified the business of eradicating the Catholic branch of the Stuart dynasty, for many of those who helped to uproot James would have been loyal to the legitimate next-in-line, had the child been there instead of on the soil of the enemy. James' flight harmed his cause so much that, when he was captured during his first attempt to get out of his kingdom, William ordered him to be set free so that he might escape to France—which he promptly proceeded to do, thus undermining any countermove that might still be mounted in his favor.

169

He, who had been too firm when he should have been conciliatory, lost his head and panicked when he probably could have salvaged much, including the throne for his son, by a display of courage. He broke so quickly, so utterly, so catastrophically, that it has been argued that his mental processes must have been sapped by disease.

The men around him were caught in the smashup of the regime. They scurried for safety. Petre managed to get across the Channel, and that was the last England was to see of him. Jeffreys tried to follow disguised in women's clothes but was discovered and incarcerated in the Tower where he died shortly afterward. Sunderland, the cunning politician, landed on his feet. Realizing that one who had been so close to James II might be overwhelmed by the rising tide of revolution before he could do anything to save himself, Sunderland crossed over to Holland and undertook to win William's favor at long range. Ostentatiously he changed his religion back to Anglicanism. To rebut the charge that he had worked for James in good faith he published an apologia, the title of which speaks for itself : *The Earl of Sunderland's Letter to a Friend in London, Plainly discovering the Designs of the Romish party and Others for the Subverting of the Protestant Religion and the Laws of the Kingdom.* He waited while his wife went to London to plead for him. The upshot was all he could have desired. Freed by an amnesty, Sunderland re-turned home, re-entered public life, proved his worth to the new regime, and eventually became an advisor to William III. Appropriately has he been called "the inextinguishable Sunderland."

The conduct of Churchill and Petre, of Jeffreys and Sunderland, covered the three things that old adherents of James II might do while the Glorious Revolution was going on : they could betray James, they could flee into exile, or they could manipulate the revolutionary circumstances in their own favor. One man of the lot refused to do any of these things — William Penn.

Penn on the Defensive

He did not leave London during the crisis, not even when the Dutch forces sent ahead by William of Orange entered the city. At that point, no more than anyone else could Penn foresee how the turmoil would end; and even when the outlines of a permanent transformation became apparent, he remained where he was. Always brave enough to face animosity, always convinced of his own rectitude, he did not consider the danger to himself sufficient to call for any dramatic move on his part. He probably imagined that he would be left in peace after a few questions.

If so, he miscalculated very seriously. He had long been under suspicion by Whigs and Anglicans. William had known him as a spokesman for James II ever since their meeting at The Hague to discuss religious equality for England. William had contradicted Penn then. Now he ordered him to be put through a minute investigation.

Penn was harassed for the next four years, arrested several times, questioned by the Privy Council and by the new King himself, spending part of the time in the Tower and part of it in hiding. The *Calendar of State Papers* mentions him in terms like these :

"*22 June 1689.* Warrant to apprehend William Penn, suspected of high treason.

"*14 July 1690.* Proclamation for the apprehension for high treason of [several persons, including] William Penn, esquire.

"*4 February 1691.* Proclamation for the discovering and apprehending the late Bishop of Ely, William Penn, and James Grahame."

The general pattern of the attack on Penn could have

been predicted. Mistrusted because of his past friendship with
James II, he was accused of conspiring for a return of James
to the throne. He was said to be in correspondence with the
fallen Stuart, and advising him to come back and undo the
Glorious Revolution. There were those prepared to testify to
his conspiratorial activities: "Against the Earl of Clarendon,
Mr. Grahame and Mr. Penn there are two witnesses, which
are sufficient in law to convict them. . . ." Penn's defense
was: "I know false witnesses are rife against me both here
and in Ireland." Under cross-examination he did, of course,
freely admit his friendship with James; more, he would not
say that he had been wrong or that he thought any the less
of James for what had happened; but he did most strenu-
ously deny conniving in any way for a return of the exiled
monarch.

> I do profess solemnly in the presence of God, that I have
> no hand or share in any Conspiracy against the King or
> Government, nor do I know any that have ; and this I can
> affirme, without directing my intention equivocally.
> Let it be enough, I say, and that truly, I know of no
> invasions or insurrections, men, money, or arms, for them,
> or any juncto or consult for advice or correspondency in
> order to it. Nor have I ever met with those named as
> the members of conspiracy or prepared any measures with
> them.

What makes it difficult to doubt that Penn had been in
touch with James is the scepticism of his old friend Henry
Sidney, who reported to King William: "Mr. Penn is as
much in this business as anybody, and two of the letters are
certainly of his writing, and if we can catch him it will so
appear."

That Penn was counseling James to attack England is
much more dubious, and here his defense proved too strong
to be breached. This episode in Penn's life is explained most

reasonably by the surmise that he wrote to James while the issue between James and William was still in the balance (extending this period in his own mind after it had ended in actual fact), and that he ceased to write after the triumph of William was too obvious to be doubted any longer. In short, the Penn-James relationship in 1688-89 was probably one of correspondence but not conspiracy. That would make understandable the lingering suspicion of Penn without an indictment.

Macaulay does not accept any explanation that would exculpate Penn. The historian isolates some discredited evidence in order to allege that Penn certainly did engage in something more sinister than mere correspondence: "The return which he made for the lenity with which he had been treated does not much raise his character. Scarcely had he again begun to harangue in public about the unlawfulness of war, than he sent a message earnestly exhorting James to make an immediate descent on England with thirty thousand men."

Putting aside everything else in this paragraph, "lenity" is a strange word to use of Penn's treatment. He was hounded for an unconscionably long time by the authorities, and on very little tangible evidence. Penn lamented that "I have been above these three years hunted up and down, and could never be allowed to live quietly in City or Country." At one point he was actually accused of high treason on the testimony of the notorious professional informer William Fuller, the indignity being compounded by the fact that Fuller was not in England at the time. Penn (who had heard so many defenses of "legality" in the time of James II) protests that the procedure is an affront to English law.

But that an Englishman in England walking about the streets should have a Bill of High Treason found against him in Ireland for a fact pretended to be committed in

England, when a man cannot legally be tryed in one
County in England for a Crime committed in another—
And the others are at ease that were accused for the same
fault, and that Fuller is nationally staged and censured
for an Imposter, that was the Chief of my Accusers—my
estate in Ireland is, notwithstanding, lately put among
the Estates of Outlaws to be leased for the Crown, and
the Collector of the Hundred where it lyes ordered to seize
my Rents and lease it in the name of the Government, and
yet I am not convicted or outlawed.

Because of this experience Penn ever after emphasized the
control of informers as an essential part of good government.

He had been appealing to his old acquaintances who were
in power in the Williamite administration, some of whom
were beholden to him for favors done only a few years, or
months, before. In desperation he now requested Henry Sidney to meet him secretly for a man-to-man discussion of the
treason charges. Sidney came, listened, and then wrote to the
King: "It would be too long for you to read a full account
of our discourse, but in short it was this: that he was a true
and faithful servant to King William and Queen Mary, and
if he knew anything that was prejudicial to them or their
government, he would readily discover it."

Penn would not, however, condescend to accept a royal
pardon. Once he had interceded with James for John Locke,
only to have Locke reject the proffered clemency on the
ground that he had done nothing wrong. The Glorious Revolution gave Locke a somewhat similar position close to the
throne, and the philosopher offered to repay his debt in kind
by wangling a royal pardon for Penn from William. To this
Penn replied as Locke had: no crime having been committed, no pardon could be appropriate. Nor would Penn
consider withdrawing to Pennsylvania as a face-saving solution: "I will not receive my liberty to go as a condition to go

there, and be there as here looked on as an article exile." In the end he got what he asked for — full exoneration.

There is no reason to question Penn's word when he calls himself "a true and faithful servant to King William and Queen Mary." That he expressed gratitude to James II and defended James' reign did not compromise his belief that the allegiance of subjects in a state overtaken by revolution belongs to the man who happens to be sitting on the throne. Penn would have preferred to see James on the English throne. James being gone, William having taken his place, then to William would Penn give his undivided fealty. He did not become a Jacobite. He did not work for the restoration of James II : he might have done so had there been legal means at his disposal, but armed intervention was all he could look for, and nothing in his biography implies that he would have backed a possible civil war. (Noticeably, he did not join James in Ireland). Penn's quiescence during the bid of James III, the Old Pretender, to recapture the throne by force unfortunately proves nothing, for by that time — the Fifteen — Penn was a paralytic and near the end of his life.

It all comes down to this, that Penn was enough of a realist in politics to comprehend that revolutions, once successful, become, by the very fact of success, legitimate systems. His attitude to 1688 is reflected in these lines from *Richard III* :

> My Lord of Gloster, in those busy days
> Which here you urge to prove us enemies,
> We followed then our Lord, our sovereign king.
> So should we you, if you should be our king.

As soon as he admitted to himself that James was gone for good, Penn was forced to admit that friendship had become irrelevant to his duty as a subject of the Crown. Not even the most fanatical Jacobites ever accused him of being a hypocrite or a traitor because he would not join them; nor did the men raised to power by the Glorious Revolution refuse to accept his motives after his innocence of treason had been established.

Penn had practical as well as theoretical reasons for acknowledging the new order. His "interest" led him in the same direction as his political philosophy. Retirement to Saint Germain to be with James II in exile would have ruined his private affairs, hurt his family, and lost him his American province — a personal disaster he might have braved if his conscience had directed him to, but which he saw no reason to force against the dictates of prudence and common sense. His conscience told him to be frank about his loyalty to James II; it did not tell him to throw away his place in the world for the sake of a lost cause.

There was, at the same time, one other factor that ought to have exercised his moral sense a bit more. Mary and Anne were James' daughters, and the way they turned on their father scandalized less sensitive people than William Penn who, from his actions, seemed not to have been disturbed by the scene being played before his eyes.

The case of Queen Mary does not have to be stressed : she was one of those most hostile to Penn. But Queen Anne invited him back to Court, and he accepted. Why did he go? Was it relief at being on so stable a footing once again? Or the better to protect his Pennsylvania investment? Or to work again for religious equality? Or because, having enjoyed the prestige of a courtier before, he wanted to enjoy it again? Granting that all of these questions bear on the problem, did Penn's conscience never twitch ever so slightly when he was being affable with the unfilial daughter of James II?

A courtier, he could not be the confidant he had been with James. Pennsylvania occupied him more and more. In 1692 he had lost control of his colony. The suspicion of William and Mary affected the Crown's decision; but there was also the more important factor of England's involvement in the War of the League of Augsburg (King William's War), when the Quaker administration of the colony proved too pacifist for London to sanction. Two years later, the war going well, Penn regained Pennsylvania.

His second trip across the Atlantic (1699-1701) proved that he had survived his time of troubles in good spirit. He vigorously examined his Holy Experiment, noted its increase in population and wealth, agreed that its political maturity demanded a new and more democratic constitution, and granted the Charter of Privileges (1701). This visit was a triumphant success for the proprietor. It was also a warning that his colonists were becoming restive under his guiding hand. After he left for home the situation deteriorated. The three lower counties, accepting an offer he had made them, decided to form an assembly of their own, thus destroying the pristine unity of Pennsylvania. The popular movement identified with David Lloyd swelled up, insisting on greater power for the popular legislature in the running of the colony. There were quarrels about elections, courts, rents, trade.

The Holy Experiment was not going precisely as Penn had intended. He believed quite sincerely in democracy (in the broad sense) and self-government; but he believed just as sincerely in order and strong central government, and he wanted to be obeyed when he thought obedience his due— as here. He wrote a series of hortatory epistles imploring his people to stop their disputes and live in the industrious contentment he had charted for them. They were so far from heeding him that under Queen Anne he would have sold his rights to the Crown if his physical breakdown had not intervened to prevent the transfer.

Penn and the Revolution Settlement

Penn made his peace with the constitutional system introduced after the Glorious Revolution, but this is not to say that he reconciled himself to all the changes in Church and State. If he was in no position to write freely as he had under James II, his past utterances reveal what he would like to have written; and after the burden of suspicion ceased to hamper him, he even expressed mild distaste for certain developments following upon the fall of James. As far as Penn was concerned, 1688-and-after divided into three elements : (1) things he could accept as such; (2) things he made himself accept in default of something better; and (3) things he could not accept at all.

(1). He was relieved to see order rather than anarchy arrive with William of Orange and his Dutch troops. Civil war did not break out. The Revolution Settlement was introduced without violence or the mass proscription of the defeated. England very soon returned to normal under the moderation of William III. Scotland and Ireland did not share this good fortune; but Penn never had much to do with Scotland, while, in spite of his close ties with Ireland, in spite of his humanitarianism, he remained throughout his life curiously indifferent to the oppression of the Irish (except the Irish Quakers).

A substantial part of the Bill of Rights was in harmony with Penn's political philosophy. He had no reason to object to limited monarchy (he had never believed in the divine right of kings); or to the codification of the place of Parliament in the national government (he had staunchly defended the rights of Parliament from law and history); or to the decision on periodical elections (he had always felt that under a tolerable government there has to be some method of consulting the people).

The new status of the King left Penn unalarmed. In salient ways William III looked very much like James II— challenging the authority of Parliament, using the veto to turn aside legislation, holding stiffly in his own hands the guiding lines of foreign policy and war. The real difference between the two men was not in their concepts of kingship but in their personalities and positions. James was generally unyielding, William conciliatory. James, descended from the legitimate dynasty, could not and would not make concessions that came naturally to a foreigner invited to England to perform a specific function. Penn did not cavil at William's political behavior.

On the ecclesiastical side, the Toleration Act would have been acceptable to Penn insofar as it ruled out physical persecution of the sects and set forth specific regulations by which non-Anglicans could be secured from the revival of past attempts to exterminate them. A privileged place for the Church of England was something that he had proposed several times as a matter of common sense expediency.

(2). Penn, like many other Englishmen, was willing to have a Dutch king in default of a more satisfactory candidate for the throne. If he preferred the sovereign who had inherited the throne legitimately according to the historical experience of England and the time-honored tradition of the English nation, he had never let conventional usage dictate to morality or prudence; and, all things being equal, he need not jibe at a foreigner wielding the scepter. The Dutch angle would not have offended Penn : he was himself half Dutch.

The end to the suspending power of the Crown removed a royal prerogative that Penn had always regarded as a necessary bulwark of English liberties. He did not want this part of the Bill of Rights. He could console himself to this extent, that the dispensing power remained, although the way James had used it was denounced. If the King could not now

declare null and void Parliamentary decisions contravening
the natural law, he could at least hold up such decisions
instead of standing by while they went into effect. A lot still
depended on the King. William was never as tolerant as
James, but he was no persecutor; and for that Penn was
grateful.

Perhaps Penn pinned his hopes on the rule of law, looking
for a written constitution such as the one he had given Pennsylvania. He might have waited to see if, the crisis petering
out, a better law on freedom of conscience and basic human
rights would be forthcoming. Any hope of this nature was
deferred from year to year, religious equality never emerged
from the Revolution Settlement, and when Penn died the
Toleration Act was still in force. In his time Dissenters and
Catholics knew only sufferance without complete freedom
of worship.

(3). The things Penn opposed in the Revolution Settlement are clearest of all. They were things he had been
opposing, resolutely and volubly, since back in the reign of
Charles II.

He lamented the crushing weight of Whig and Anglican
supremacy that in 1688 descended on his country. England
was to be, basically, Whig in politics and Anglican in religion
— exactly the balance of power he had striven so hard to
prevent.

Penn thought the new order got off on the wrong foot at
the start when it indicted James II for a persecuting tyrant.
The principal clause of the indictment in the Bill of Rights
begins with this preamble: "Whereas the late King James
the Second, by the assistance of divers evil counsellors, judges
and ministers employed by him, did endeavour to subvert
and extirpate the Protestant religion and the laws and liberties
of this kingdom. . . ."

The accusation collided with every stand Penn had taken,

with everything he had said and written. Answering Halifax
and others, Penn had roundly denied that James ever
threatened "the laws and liberties of this kingdom." Even his
misfortunes during the Glorious Revolution could not make
him stammer when his previous assertions about James were
alleged against him. Penn did not concur that James had
proven Catholic monarchs unfit to govern the Protestant
realm of England. How could he, when he had repeatedly
stated that freedom might best be safeguarded by a Catholic
monarch working with, or against, a Protestant legislature?

Penn looked more favorably on the Bill of Rights than on
the Toleration Act. The former, in his opinion, insulted and
slandered James to a degree; but its positive platform did not
shock him unduly. The Toleration Act did shock him by
bringing his worst fears into reality.

His proposed three-cornered balance of Anglicans, Dissenters, and Catholics went into the discard. The Anglicans
became dominant. The Dissenters and Catholics became
second-class citizens. The Test Act remained in force along
with the penal laws. To understand what this meant to Penn
consider these two paragraphs, one from James II's Declaration of Indulgence, the other from the Toleration Act.

Declaration of Indulgence. We do likewise declare that
it is our royal will and pleasure that from henceforth
the execution of all and all manner of penal laws in matters
ecclesiastical, for not coming to Church or not receiving
the sacrament, or for any other nonconformity to the
religion established, or for or by reason of the exercise of
religion in any manner whatsoever, be immediately suspended ; and the further execution of the said penal laws
and every of them is hereby suspended.

Toleration Act. Provided always, and be it further
enacted by the authority aforesaid, that neither this Act,
nor any clause, article, or thing herein contained, shall
extend or be construed to extend to give any ease, benefit,

or advantage to any papist or popish recusant whatsoever, or any person that shall deny in his preaching or writing the doctrine of the blessed Trinity, as it is declared in the aforesaid Articles of Religion.

Catholics and Unitarians were therefore excluded from the leniency extended to other Englishmen. Penn would have excluded neither. His feeling about the Catholics offers no problem. His feeling about the Unitarians was less simple. He sympathized with those radicals who disliked the orthodox creed, and he thought they had a right to speak freely. At the same time he himself in his theory and practice withholds from non-Christians their political rights. The upshot would seem to be that he agreed with the Toleration Act insofar as it punished Unitarians who rejected the divinity of Christ and that he disagreed with it in its treatment of Unitarians willing to call themselves Christians.

Protestant Dissenters were not dealt with as harshly as the Catholics and Unitarians. They were, nonetheless, severely restrained in their acts and ambitions by the statutes aimed at keeping out of public life those who refused to conform to the Church of England. The bare right of other faiths to exist in the English state was itself under constant assault by bigoted Anglicans, and all non-Anglicans lived in perpetual jeopardy of fresh penal laws that might be voted by Parliament.

William Penn, therefore, still had work to do. He could not now press for full religious equality, which no one in power wanted after 1688. He could not bring up to date and reissue publications like his *Great Case of Liberty of Conscience* (1670) and his *Great and Popular Objection against the Repeal of the Penal Laws and Tests* (1688). All he could do was to labor for the maximum of liberty within the framework of legalized inequality. This he did with all the resources still remaining to him.

During the reign of William and Mary he resumed his role of spokesman for the Quakers. When it seemed as if Parliament might impose the oath of allegiance on the Quakers in spite of the Toleration Act, Penn wrote a paper defining the position of the Society of Friends and presented it to the House of Commons. In it he said of his co-religionists that "they humbly hope that, being to suffer for untruth as for perjury, their request will not be uneasy, since they subject their integrity to trial upon the hazard of a conviction that is so much greater than the offence in the eye of the law would bear. Let them then, we pray, speak in their own way, and, if false, be punished in yours."

Three years later Parliament was debating the question of how far Nonconformist authors ought to be allowed to go in criticizing the creed of Anglican orthodoxy. The subject was calculated to touch Penn to the quick. His first experience with a prison cell had resulted from the theological opinions expressed in his *Sandy Foundation Shaken* (1668). Ever since he had been under fire, accused of being a Socinian, an Arian, a deist. Many of his writings had been, were, and would be for years into the future, defensive. Some of his titles make the theme of the controversy self-evident: *The Christian Quaker* (1674); *Primitive Christianity Revived in the Faith and Practice of the People Called Quakers* (1696); *The Quaker a Christian* (1698).

Now, in 1698, he came forward to support the right of non-Anglicans to discuss with some freedom the theology of the Bible as compared with that of the establishment. He wrote *Some Considerations upon the Bill for the more Effectual Suppressing Blasphemy and Prophaneness: Humbly Offered*, repeating therein that there is no Scriptural warrant for the Nicene Creed, the Trinitarian dogma, although insisting that the theory of the Trinity may still be accepted as scriptural if it is reduced to the simple formula of "the Three

Who bear witness in Heaven." Penn's words are milder, his argument the very minimum of what he thought must be said; but in substance it is just the kind of incipient Unitarianism that had got him into trouble thirty years before. Briefly: "Seeing the Holy Scriptures of the Old and New Testaments are confessed to be of Divine Authority, as being given by Inspiration from God: How can it be consistent with such Confession to impose a Creed in Unscriptural Terms by a Penal Act?"

Under Queen Anne, with the Occasional Conformity Bill up for discussion in Parliament, Penn came to the rescue of those Dissenters who got around the penal laws by perfunctory appearances at Church of England ceremonies, which certified them as Anglicans, and then went back to their old sectarianism no longer barred from public office. Penn did not care for hypocrisy or cowardice of this sort, but he cared much less for the system from which it sprang and was fearful of the increased tension that would result should the measure under debate be passed. To help defeat it he wrote *Considerations upon the Bill against Occasional Conformity* (1702).

Whatever effect Penn may have had on the religious laws cannot be determined. Great claims have been made for him; but we do not know whether he was really a critical force in his defense of the Quakers' affirmation and his opposition to the blasphemy act, in both of which cases his opinion was the same as the one that prevailed, or whether he did indeed contribute something to holding up the Occasional Conformity Bill, so that it did not pass Parliament until the "Tory reaction" of Queen Anne's later reign. We *do* know that Penn did not like the condition of religion in England during the years from 1688 until his death in 1718.

(There is no contradiction in the fact that he led a Quaker delegation to thank Queen Anne for promising to continue her support of the Toleration Act. By that time the choice lay between persecution and partial freedom, and naturally he chose the latter. But under James II there had been a third option — complete freedom.)

For Penn to promote another Declaration of Indulgence was out of the question. Even intercession in behalf of individuals had become difficult. Under James II, Penn had wangled a pardon for John Locke. Under Queen Anne, Penn failed to wangle a pardon for Daniel Defoe.

Defoe presents an ironic spectacle. No Englishman had opposed James II more bitterly, or more enthusiastically welcomed William III. Defoe had attacked the one and defended the other with his pen. Like Halifax, he was the author of a *Letter to a Dissenter* (1688) in which he ridiculed the idea that James might be sincere about religious freedom, and demanded rigid enforcement of the anti-Catholic laws. Defoe admired Halifax, with whose politics he expressed fundamental agreement.

Yet time had not vindicated the argument put forward by Halifax to prove the recently-acquired magnanimity of the Church of England; and one man who might have testified to this from personal experience was Daniel Defoe.

Since Defoe was a Dissenter, he hardly profited from the Revolution Settlement, except that his pet aversion, James II, was gone. If Defoe rejoiced in the fate of the Catholics under the Toleration Act, he did not rejoice in the fate of the Dissenters. He felt in his own person the crippling handicap of the pro-Anglican laws and, like Penn, feared that worse was to come. That was the background to Defoe's famous satire *The Shortest Way with the Dissenters* (1702), in which he pretended to advocate the hanging of Protestant Nonconformists as the best solution the Anglicans could find to the intransigence of these non-Anglicans.

Provoked by the same Parliamentary debate that provoked

Penn's *Considerations upon the Bill against Occasional Conformity*, Defoe's pamphlet fooled the "high flyers" of the establishment who were inclined to agree with an argument they could not realize to be a tongue-in-cheek affair. By the same token, Defoe horrified and terrified the Dissenters who did not see through the satire. The result was notoriety for the author — and a sentence to the pillory.

The circumstances under which Penn met Defoe are unknown. No great mutual interests could have attracted them: they had little enough in common beyond non-Anglican Protestantism. The austere Quaker contrasted with the raffish journalist, undercover agent, and author of *Robinson Crusoe*. Their opinions of James II were flatly incompatible. Defoe did not, as Penn did, believe in freedom of conscience even for Catholics. They came together just this once because Defoe was suffering for his religion (although politics were mixed up in it), and Penn could never resist the moral claims of such a case.

Penn spoke for Defoe at Court, then wrote to Godolphin: "I beg this man's disgrace may be deferr'd if not pardoned." The reply was negative. Defoe stood in the pillory. He was not the only victim to come to Penn's attention and to stir in Penn memories of James II and the Declaration of Indulgence.

The period 1688-1718 (from the Glorious Revolution to Penn's death) did not produce, rather made impossible, the national equilibrium of forces he had described as his ideal. He had to struggle against bigotry triumphant, with Whitehall as well as Parliament defending it, without so much as a glimmer in the distance of religious equality. He lived to see the surge of Anglican and Tory power symbolized by the trial of Dr. Sacheverell, who preached against toleration, was impeached, became a hero to the London mob when he entered court, and received a sentence so light as to amount to a vindication (1710). The next year the Occasional Conformity Bill was voted into law.

Penn was past protesting, almost past caring: in 1712 his stroke removed him from the arena. The "last four years of Queen Anne" and the coming of the Hanoverians passed him by. Lytton Strachey might have described for us the ideas that flitted through the invalid's mind as, in his fitful moments of rationality, he went back over the events, hopes, triumphs and failures in which he had participated, or of which he had been a spectator — the Restoration and the reign of James II and the Glorious Revolution, the trials of the Seven Bishops and Dr. Sacheverell, the Declarations of Indulgence and the Toleration Act and the Occasional Conformity Bill. We, with no entree into thoughts Penn never expressed, must be content to leave in place the veil that covers his final six years.

9

PENN'S "NAIVETE"

PENN'S PERSONAL relations with James caused him to write that the King was a man of "Grace and Goodness," of "Humility, Plainness and Courage," and, at bottom, of "Integrity." Similar epithets scattered through his works leave no conceivable doubt about his opinion. He thought very highly of the moral qualities of James Stuart. Add his political allegiance to his personal esteem, and you have the reason why Penn has been called either a fool or a knave. These, in truth, are the only possibilities, supposing him to have been wrong.

Penn's "knavery" no longer merits the dignity of refutation since nobody believes in it. Those who did believe in it have ceased to speak to us with any persuasiveness. Faith in Penn's "naïveté" is still very much alive, as may be seen in the quotations set down at the start of this book in the section entitled "*The Problem.*" Some versions of the naïveté theory are little short of nonsensical : to speak of Penn's "infantile sense of importance" is not worthy of the problem. Other versions compel examination.

If Penn was "gulled" or victimized by "credulity," this must mean one of three things. Either (1) he did not know the case against James II; or (2) he would not listen to the truth; or (3) James inveigled him into disbelieving the truth. None of these interpretations can be sustained.

(1). That Penn may not have known what was going on

at Whitehall is clearly false. He heard the chorus of maledictions rising on every side. He knew that devout Protestants, entrenched Anglicans, ambitious Whigs, cautious Tories, even moderate Catholics, all had something derogatory to say about the King. In his works he looks at the anti-James movement from almost every angle; and far from basing his counter attack on simple faith in the King, he invokes a whole body of factual information and psychological inference.

Penn has been called naïve with James just as he was naïve with Philip Ford, the steward who served him, gained control of his affairs, and then trapped him in one of the classical embezzlements of history. But there is no adequate parallel in the two cases. Ford worked for Penn over the years without causing any trouble, and like many another employer Penn was lulled into letting his trust extend too far. If some one had warned him that embezzlement was going on beneath his nose, obviously he would have set the law on Ford. Well, he *was* warned about James II.

The same response covers the case of Algernon Sidney, of whose treasonable connection with France Penn evidently never knew. Sidney was not going to broadcast the truth. He was not going to reveal it to a Quaker Royalist campaigning for him in the Parliamentary elections. That Sidney accepted French gold was a secret so well kept that its exposure caused amazement and consternation among the Whigs of the eighteenth century : "Sir John Dalrymple *(Memoirs of Great Britain and Ireland,* vol. i, 1771, Preface): When I found in the French dispatches Lord Russel intriguing with the court of Versailles, and Algernon Sidney taking money from it, I felt very near the same shock as if I had seen a son turn his back in the day of battle."

Penn's ignorance is no argument for his wide-eyed innocence with Algernon Sidney—or with James Stuart.

(2). Could it be that Penn would not listen to the truth

because he had an aversion to those who were trying to make
him see it? He can be shown to have felt disdain for many
critics who crossed swords with him on religion. The enemies
of George Fox he estimated to be men of no account; and he
could hardly be civil with Independents, Presbyterians, Anabaptists, Antinomians, Socinians. He was quite capable of self-
sophistication in his rejoinders to them. Here, in his own
words, is how he dealt with Lodowick Muggleton, a hiero-
phant of the period who put his own Inner Light above that
of the Quakers:

Penn. "Art thou the last witness that shall ever be?"

Muggleton. "Yes; and there shall never be another."

Penn. "Who sent Thee?"

Muggleton. "God spoke to John Reeve, and he spoke
to me."

Penn. "Is that all thou hast to produce, only John Reeve's
word for it? To this he avoided."

Penn was very contemptuous of Muggleton's claim to
refute George Fox. Perhaps he felt the same about the adversaries of James II? But we know this was not so. They were
often men with whom he had much in common and to whom
he was perfectly willing to listen. Sometimes he expressed
open agreement with them; sometimes, notably in the case
of Charlwood Lawton, he even brought their criticism to the
attention of the King. His defense of James II is, therefore,
utterly unlike his defense of George Fox.

(3). Finally, and most prevalent, is the idea that James
imposed on Penn's unsuspecting nature, smoothly explaining
away the crimes and vices of the regime. The first objection
that springs to mind is that Penn did not let the King explain
away either Magdalen College or the Seven Bishops. His
conduct with reference to these incidents makes it impossible
to hold simply: "Penn was naïve about James II." The
proposition has to be recast something like this: "Penn,

although a clear-headed and vocal censor of James II at some
of the most critical moments of his reign, was nevertheless
devoid of sense or suspicion on the one single issue of the
Declaration of Indulgence."

In this form the proposition will appeal to men of heroic
faith. The rest may find themselves afflicted with a crude
form of scepticism. The Declaration of Indulgence was aimed
at promoting freedom of religion? So was the attack on
Magdalen College. The attempt to pack Parliament tampered
with existing positive law? So did the Declaration of Indulgence. If Penn was gullible about the Declaration of Indulgence, he should have been gullible about Magdalen College.
If he criticized the attempt to pack Parliament, he should
have criticized the Declaration of Indulgence, granted that
the same principle was involved. The conclusion can only be
that he looked at all three cases with open eyes and decided
on reasonable grounds that, different principles being involved, James was wrong about two of them and right about
the third.

Again, James has not often been accused of being smooth
in his dealings with other men; he was actually rash and
stubborn, incapable of finesse or diplomatic intrigue, the
precise opposite of Charles II (as Charles realized and said,
mourning in advance the fate he suspected must be his
brother's).

Shall we say that Penn knew a different James, a wily,
velvety James, a James who could exploit him alone of all
men? If so, the King may have been using Penn. But the
King has himself been thought to have been systematically
deceived and abused by Sunderland. The school of thought
that holds to this notion and to the one above as well would
have us believe that while James was using Penn, Sunderland
was using *him*. Then there is the possibility that Petre was
using Sunderland. . . .

In the world of common sense, Penn could not have been imposed upon as the theory would have it. There is no iron logic in the inference that just because he was so passionately attached to religious equality he put his mind in his pocket when surveying the Declaration of Indulgence. There is as much reason to argue that just because he was so passionately attached to religious equality he was ever on guard to unmask hypocrisy. With the King's motives under fire, Penn could not have avoided judging them in the most serious way, and he did so judge them for the benefit of his readers when writing of the reign. It would be absurd to try to absolve him of any error or sophistry in his thought about his monarch, friend, and benefactor, but naïveté was denied to him by circumstances.

Penn had heard the charge of his being an instrument of his royal policies. He realized that he gave the appearance of one who had undertaken to bring the Dissenters over on the toleration issue. He would deny, not the fact, but the interpretation.

With strong convictions that the King was right, that the Declaration of Indulgence was sound and moral, naturally he was willing to speak to the Dissenters; he was anxious to speak to them. Only, he could see nothing wrong in so doing. He was acting for himself, not as a puppet, when he "magnified the King's Indulgence" in his sermons. He was happy to go to The Hague to discuss the Test Act with William of Orange. Why not? Here was another chance to work against the hated measure. The difficulty is to comprehend how anyone could ever have called him a "tool" of Stuart autocracy. He himself ruled out the absurdity by writing during the Williamite period:

I acknowledge I was an instrument to break the jaws of persecution, and to that end I once did take the freedom to remember King James of his frequent assurances in

favour of liberty of conscience, and with much zeal used
my small interest with him to gain that point upon his
ministers that he told me were against it . . . . This and
personal good offices were my daily business at Whitehall,
of which I can take the righteous God of heaven and earth
to witness. *Nor can I yet see that providence of liberty
and peace, which we enjoyed under him, was such a trick
or snare as some have represented it.*

Penn lived for thirty years after the Glorious Revolution,
survived, although doting, into the reign of George I (when
the malignity of James II had long been a national dogma),
and went to his grave with his faith in James still intact. This
being so, on the "naïveté" hypothesis he must have been a
moral and intellectual buffoon — which we know he was not.

It should not go unmentioned that there were others besides
Penn, and not only Jacobites, who received a favorable impression of James. William Mead, who accompanied Penn to
the 1673 meeting with the Duke of York, and who had no
personal link with the royal family, declared his "extreme
satisfaction" with what James said about religious toleration
in general and about the Friends specifically. The Quaker
theologian Robert Barclay "never found reason to doubt his
sincerity in the matter of liberty of conscience." It was James'
old antagonist, Bishop Burnet, who remarked of him: "In a
word, if it had not been for his popery, he would have been,
if not a great, yet a good prince."

Penn was *not* naive about James II as man and monarch.
Was he overly-optimistic about the royal policies and their
chances for success? Did he underestimate the rage and determination of those committed to stopping the King at all costs?
Did he rely too much on logic and morality to weaken
psychological and sociological pressures?

He did; and it was his worst mistake. His distaste for the
Church of England — the arch-persecutor of the Quakers —

made him too receptive to James' plan for raising up non-Anglicans as a counterweight to the establishment. Concentrating on the mathematics of justice and the alleviation of suffering, Penn could not feel for the Anglican ecclesiastics who viewed the future of their church with increasing alarm. He could not sympathize with their conclusion that ruin would be their lot should they allow James II to go on. *Penn* talked of tolerant Catholic sovereigns; *they* saw with single-eyed intensity the intolerance of the Catholic sovereign of France. *He* said the King wanted to maintain the Church of England; *they* felt the King's heavy hand on the dioceses and the universities. *He* addressed himself to men of moderate good sense; *they* were men too frightened to listen. Places and privileges they had already lost under James II by 1688, and they were resolved to lose no more.

Two things have to be carefully distinguished — the condition of England as an objective fact, and the condition of England as an image inside the heads of James' adversaries. Penn misunderstood the power of the image to becloud the fact. He thought it sufficient to prove that his country could safely permit toleration to the Catholics and that to do so would be political good sense. He had no inkling that men suffering from neurosis develop psychological rigidities that keep them impervious to reality or reason. He could have perceived more clearly the nature of the attacks on James had he related them to the attacks on himself : he was denounced for a Catholic and a Jesuit; and if a well-known Quaker leader could be accused of disseminating Romanist propaganda, then it followed that the distrust of a genuinely Catholic ruler must have been profound and irremediable.

It was one of those eras of history when the hardest of facts is mass feeling. Those English Catholics realized this who preferred to accept discrimination (and peace) when Penn was asking justice for them. Twentieth century America has a mild parallel in the Catholics who prefer not to see a Catholic President because, their civil and religious rights being guaranteed, they don't want to rouse animosity among anti-Catholics who believe that "America would be run by the Pope." If this kind of thinking can flourish today, how much stronger must it have been in the days when England was racked by religious tensions?

The real question was not whether James was going to take his politics from Rome or summon the French army or close Parliament, but whether so many Englishmen believed it, and with so much fear and hatred, as to render unwise James' bid for freedom of conscience and full citizenship for all. No one is prepared any longer to say that the majority of the people of England wanted to dethrone their King; the majority would, if consulted, have declared for James II as a matter of course, for seventeenth century rebellions were not started by democratic voting procedures, and especially not in an England that remembered what had happened the last time a sovereign was overthrown. A few powerful magnates leading a determined minority and assisted by the apathy of the bulk of the people — these made the Glorious Revolution. Sir Charles Petrie says that "The Revolution was the work of a minority and of a comparatively small minority at that. It was not the result of a national rising against a hated and tyrannical monarch, for, as has been said, had James kept his head, he might have kept his crown as well. It was rather due to a discontented faction, more powerful than numerous, which found an energetic and capable leader, and achieved its purposes by rapidity of its movements."

Was Penn wrong to challenge this "discontented faction" by supporting the Declaration of Indulgence? To say so would be a hard saying. His was no case of blind stupidity. He underestimated the forces arrayed against him; but he was not unaware that real opposition existed, and he faced it in the knowledge that he could not win without a struggle. Morally, he had little choice: he could not offend his conscience by retreating from his principle of freedom of worship for everybody, or from his duty to defend the principle publicly. Even after the explosion of 1688, when he was being harassed by William and Mary, he still thought and said that he had chosen the right path. Failure for him was better than not to try.

The failure, moreover, was not foredoomed. *We* know what the outcome was, but this is hindsight and therefore irrelevant. If William won and James lost, the antecedent hazard was that the reverse would happen; for William won on a terrific gamble, and James lost on a lesser one. The whole politico-ecclesiastical situation of 1685–88 was such that James might have kept his throne in spite of everything. *If* he had been persuaded to slow down when resentment over his rule was beginning to turn into hot anger, *if* his son had been born either before or after the crisis of the Seven Bishops, *if* he had stayed to fight William instead of losing his head and bolting into exile—"ifs" like these are amusing to later generations, but they were living realities at the time and prove how the incalculable upset Penn's political reasoning. It is arguable that he was quite correct according to the fact as he knew them. It is certain that he dealt with a complex of persons and events much too tangled for any man to grasp, let alone unravel. But he was as close to being right as anyone.

The negative criticism of Penn would be closer to the nub if he had been the only man in England to speak of James II as he did. The truth is that many allies were joined with him, the literature of the time being full of parallels to his own pamphlets. It is conceivable that Penn did not invent any one of the arguments he employed, except when speaking of his personal experience. They were common coin on the pro-James side of the fence. The following excerpts may be taken

as typical of what Penn's allies were saying. The excerpts
corroborate three of Penn's principal theses : the constancy
of James II as a proponent of religious toleration, the respon-
sibility of the Church of England for quareling with the King,
and the safety for the nation that would come of Parliament
backing the King on toleration :

> I might here add many other Considerations to dissipate
> this panic Fear. As, The Spirit of the Nation, now anim-
> ated more than ever against Popery. The Interest of the
> Papists themselves to keep within modest and moderate
> Bounds, lest too great stretching after things out of their
> Reach, should make them lose their present Footing. And,
> not improperly, The Word of a King, who has solemnly
> promised us that he will not suffer any Man to be oppressed
> in the just Liberty of his Conscience : Of a King, I say,
> who does not now first begin to affect that language, but
> who has been long known to assert the same Principle.
> You will say, perhaps, the consequences of that connivance,
> and the enlargement of his favours to Roman Catholicks
> ever since, has but too much excused and even justified our
> suspicion then ; but, now, we the well-meaning men of our
> Party are apt to blame it the more ; for 'tis not the first
> time that unreasonable Jealousie has produced the very
> thing suspected ; and besides, we had but little cause to
> grudge at his shewing inclination to his own Principles,
> when in all essential matters he complied with ours.
>
> Whereas if the Toleration is General, and All Recusants,
> as well the Protestant as Roman Catholic, *equally* compre-
> hended in the Grant thereof, in one Act, and upon one
> Bottom, a Consideration of the Quality, the Number, and
> the Interests of the Parties so joyned together in the Liberty,
> will secure the Possession of it in Future.
>
> There may be Laws made and Incorporated into the very
> Body of the Bill of Abolition, that may prevent a Popish
> Parliament as much as a Presbyterian Parliament for ever

being Chosen, unless the Protestants do choose them themselves, that is, the most part of them.

Penn was not a single gladiator standing out against an army and challenging all comers. He was the most significant figure of a significant group — the pro-James non-Catholics. The more closely he is set into this ideological background, the more dubious does his naïveté become; for too many other witnesses have to be stigmatized as naive along with him. The hypothesis ought to be entertained that these were the true realists of the period, and that the anti-James pamphleteers were naïve.

One added point. Penn might have appealed to a feckless pacifism, but never did. He never argued that James II should have his way because it was the duty of his subjects to obey without protest. Some Church of England men defended this procedure, as James expected them to do because of their reiterated principle about non-resistance to the Crown (the principle that originated as a shield of the English Reformation against the Papacy). These individuals condemned the opposition to James II for being wrong as such. Not so William Penn. He defended obedience for a different reason, namely that he considered James, not a bad King who should be obeyed because of an abstract theory of government, but a good King who should be obeyed because of a worthy end toward which he was working.

10

PENN, JAMES
AND THE HISTORIANS

PENN'S IS the ablest defense of James II ever written. He was the ideal man for the task, for no one else stood on a vantage-ground so strategic for a realistic investigation of the King's acts and intentions. Penn was neither a Catholic like Petre, nor an anti-Catholic like Halifax, nor a suspect convert to Catholicism like Sunderland. He was not tied to the Court like Jeffreys or separated from the Court like Burnet. His expressed convictions are neither invariably favorable to the King nor systematically derogatory; and from the multitude of writings he published of other subjects, from his political and religious career, we know he was an honest and knowledgeable man. Although emotionally committed to most of the royal policies, he could not afford the luxury of wishful thinking : his brief for James II is drawn up with the sceptics in mind; and so he supports it was as many facts as he can gather and with reasoning tested at every step of the syllogism.

Why has he been so signally unsuccessful in persuading his readers to accept his brief? His failure is inscribed in big letters across the scholarship devoted to him. Even the Quaker historians have never come out four-square for him. Despite the veneration with which they write of the greatest man ever to join their faith, not one has ever said in plain words that Penn was justified in adhering as he did to the cause of James II. Respectful and reverent about most things in Penn's life (Pennsylvania, Quakerism, the Penn–Mead trial), they suddenly become confused, hesitant, and abashed when they reach his years with James Stuart. Anxious to absolve Penn of Macaulay's allegations about the Bloody Assize and Magdalen College, they begin to falter before Penn's opinion of James. They will, in defiance of the evidence before them, dscribe the Penn–James relationship in terms that Penn would not have accepted. This is from Hull : "James had already begun the appointment of Catholics to public office, and Penn evidently approved of this; but he continued to warn the king in their private interviews of the necessity of getting parliamentary sanction for both religious toleration and political appointments." The word "warn" is inadmissible. Penn and James were of the same opinion about the need of having the concurrence of Parliament; and they were of the same opinion that the King should employ the suspending power in favor of religious toleration, whether or not Parliament ever would concur. Hull gives enough data to prove this.

Many a non-Quaker historian has been just as careless. Lord Acton, who calls Penn the "greatest historic figure of the age" and who has a reputation for being nearly infallible on modern history, completely misunderstands the cooperation of Penn and James : "It was no secret that James was resolved to be master, and to abolish the restraints and safeguards of the constitution. Penn, reporting his intentions to William of Orange, declared he would have all or nothing." But the context to which Acton refers reveals beyond cavil that "all or nothing" had to do specifically with religious toleration, with James asking William to declare against the Test Act and not merely against the other penal laws. It is a perversion of the truth to imply that Penn, in his mission to The Hague, was bent on helping James "to abolish the restraints and safeguards of the constitution." And to whom was James' evil intent "no secret"? To Penn—who testified so clearly that no such intent existed?

The historians of every period have tended to treat Penn's conduct with indulgence at best, contempt at worst. Yet when you examine their negations you find that they never meet Penn on his own ground. They disparage James' motives with astonishing self-confidence — and without proving that they know more about these than his friend of many years. They claim James "wasn't interested in" toleration for any group except the Catholics — but never show just why we should believe them rather than the Quaker who certainly, and by common consent, was "interested in" toleration for everybody. They denounce James' "tyranny" — and bypass Penn's contention that this was a political impossibility.

Trevelyan says of James II — flatly, categorically, dogmatically — that "it was only when the breach with Episcopacy drove him to dissemble, that he took into his mouth Penn's noble doctrine of universal Toleration." Penn, however, as we have seen, tells us exactly the reverse. The very heart of his defense of James is the latter's faithful adherence over the years to the principle that consciences should be free. Penn says that he has long been acquainted with James Stuart, first as Duke of York and then as King, and has uniformly found him an advocate of toleration theoretically, and always willing to act on the theory by favoring the persecuted of other religions than his own. The record runs from 1673 to 1688, a very impressive record in Penn's judgment.

In another place Trevelyan states: "Largely at Penn's instigation, though certainly not in Penn's spirit, James issued the two Declarations of Indulgence." Still, Penn was satisfied that his "spirit" and the King's coincided nearly enough, and he might be presumed to know something about it.

Turner is quite right to call the Penn–James friendship "inexplicable." On his premises it *is* inexplicable. Those historians like Trevelyan who accept the same premises and still attempt an explanation merely succeed in becoming intellectually incoherent. The only alternative is to say with Macaulay that Penn was a conniving rascal, and this no one is willing to do any longer.

The problem of Penn turns on the problem of James. The radical good will of the former cannot subsist with the radical malevolence of the latter. Our opinion of one of them has to change, and the significant thing is that it is our opinion of the King that is changing. Today historians are more willing to say a good word for James II than they have ever been before. Ironically, the Quaker scholars who were in a splendid position to force the change never did so. They never challenged the non-Quakers in these terms : "Our version of Penn being correct, it follows that your version of James is incorrect." The pro-Penn authors let themselves be imposed on by the anti-James pundits. With the fresh treatment of James that has emerged in the past generation (as a result of straightforward historical research, and with no intention of vindicating Penn) the most laudatory advocates of Penn might consider upgrading him.

Butterfield struck the Whig interpretation of history a damaging blow with his book on the subject; and his analysis is valid for the Whig interpretation of James II, which belongs to the pathology of historiography. From Burnet to Trevelyan the historians of the old school vested this sovereign with incompatible qualities and judged him by criteria that would turn almost any figure of modern history into a melodramatic villain. James is portrayed as the man of arbitrary rule who strives to get his personal acts legalized by Parliament; the flinty, dictatorial despot yearning to kiss the slipper of the King of France; the extreme Romanist who ignores the Pope; the savage persecutor who invariably speaks in defense of universal toleration; the vengeful nurser of grudges who pardons Whig opponents like John Locke. James is the individual who is wrong no matter what he does; so if he appears to be doing something inherently good and right, then he obviously has a sinister ulterior motive.

This analysis of James produced as a by-product the portrayal of Penn as a psychological freak of an analogous kind. Penn becomes the Quaker leader and preacher who supports a Quaker-hating Romanist; the protagonist of religious toleration who would have caused the death of toleration had his plans succeeded; the statesman of freedom who works for a despot; the man who goes to jail in the name of English liberties and backs a royal policy aimed directly at putting an end to those liberties; the urgent critic, and at the same time the credulous victim, of James II. Penn is the good and wise empire-builder in Pennsylvania who somehow undergoes a transmogrification when he enters Whitehall.

No one has ever drawn these two men in such stark terms; the contradictions would have been too evident; but the elements all exist implicitly and between the lines, while an astounding number are explicitly stated. To the examples already noted we may add as a summation this headlong flight from reality : "No two men could have been more flatly unlike each other. There was James with his green, supercilious face, the mask of cruelty and weakness; and there was Penn, softly important, a rounded, parsonic figure (though only forty-one), an elderly cherub in a round hat, beaming with idealised humanity." If that is the case for the prosecution, then the defense may rest with some confidence in the verdict.

The old interpretation of James II was so faulty that it broke down even in the hands of writers by no means inclined to serve as apologists for James. Thus Seeley, an enthusiastic hater of this sovereign, confesses that James "anticipated modern liberalism in proclaiming the inalienable rights of conscience and in announcing the abandonment of all penal laws." A later scholar says of James that "He had a respect for law and the authority of parliament with which he is not usually credited. He suspended certain statutes, but he never pretended to abrogate them, and when he thought of suspending the second Test Act in 1687, and Sunderland told him, rather whiggishly, that it would be unconstitutional to tamper with a statute defining the composition of parliament, he agreed docilely enough."

So after all the sound and fury, James II emerges as what Penn insisted he was — a believer in religious toleration and English liberties. Another historian of our time remarks of James' religious policy:

> The solution would be easier if one could accept the claim, so often made, that James was trying to force the people of England to become Roman Catholics. That accusation, however, can be validated only on the assumption that every one of his own assertions to the contrary was a deliberate lie, for he himself insisted that his aim was religious toleration for those of all faiths, including Protestant Dissenters no less than Roman Catholics. Although among his followers were a number of Jesuit zealots who may have hoped for the exclusive victory of their own Church, at no point is it possible to find unquestionable proof that James agreed with them. Like most people of his own time and a good many of our own, he believed in the theory of the Oecumenical Church and hoped that the schisms of the Reformation might be healed, but he wanted this to come about through conviction or conversion rather than through force. Appalled by the Revocation of the Edict of Nantes, he believed that Louis XIV had injured the cause of Roman Catholicism by this rash act."

The author of this passage draws the conclusion to which all the logic of the case points: "Perhaps one of the best pieces of evidence to his tolerance is the fact that one of his most wholehearted supporters was the Quaker William Penn, surely astute enough to know whether or not his master's policies were a mere mask." Q. E. D.

How shall we visualise the life, career and tragedy of James II? The most authoritative expert on the subject, Sir George Clark, finds that James' downfall was "due to his virtues as well as to his vices," and in explaining this absolves him of one of the worst of the old charges, treasonable intrigue with Louis XIV : "There is no real reason to doubt the sincerity of his own subsequent professions that he never intended to subordinate British to French interests, and that, even when the general war came in sight, he thought he could keep out of it and allow England as a neutral to grow rich by trade as she had done in the last war."

Clark pictures James as playing the game of European politics according to the rules then accepted everywhere — that is, of resorting to duplicity when he found it profitable and safe. He does not whitewash James but does reveal to us a monarch, albeit foolhardy and bemused, far short of the criminal autocrat of the Whig caricature.

One historian of the newer criticism, Sir Charles Petrie, sums up the reign of James II in a formula that might almost be based explicitly on the writings and career of William Penn : "Let it be frankly admitted that the Government of James was tactless and weak, even if its objects were highly commendable, but to say that it was tyrannical or unpatriotic is absurd."

This same scholar even raises the query of how much we really know about James II after almost three centuries of condemnation.

That the faults of James have had more attention from historians than his virtues cannot be denied, and the reason is not far to seek. His cause received so much support that more than half a century after he had lost his throne his grandson came within an ace of recovering it, and thus it was a matter of life and death for the Whigs to denigrate his memory. He was depicted as a veritable ogre, and the adherents of the Hanoverian regime never tired of denouncing the terrible state of affairs which was supposed to have existed while he was on the throne, as may be seen in *Tom Jones.* The last monarch of a fallen dynasty is always treated in this manner, and writers under the Tudors so blackened the character of Richard III that to this day we do not know what manner of man he really was.

If it is possible for a contemporary scholar to write thus of James II, then surely the time has come to stop apologizing for William Penn's behavior during that sovereign's reign. It is not a question of claiming boldly that the Whig historians have done to James II what the Tudor historians did to Richard III. It *is* a question of asserting that, with the historians now divided on James, we are free to interpret Penn in a very favorable sense instead of automatically seeking for reasons why he miscalculated so atrociously.

The wheel doubtless will never circle around and come to rest precisely on the spot where Penn stands; but if a revised version of James II is to carry any kind of versimilitude, it will have to make terms with the Quaker statesman who was the first to speak out authoritatively against the caricature that has done duty for so long.

THE SOLUTION

"Penn was loyal to James II, which makes him either a fool or a knave." This first of the three possible alternatives will not stand up under analysis. "Penn was loyal to James II, but there were extenuating circumstances." This second alternative, if more specious in form, actually reduces to the first. There were no extenuating circumstances if James was a bigoted despot, an unscrupulous enemy of religious toleration and political freedom, and moreover a powerful ruler with the real capacity to turn his subjects into slaves. How could anyone but a fool have believed that a man of this type would maintain liberty once he had the chance to destroy it? How could anyone but a knave have undertaken to help him?

"Penn was loyal to James II, and he was right." This third alternative is the one we are left with.

It needs to be closely defined. It does not deny the folly of James. It does not commit us to an acceptance of everything Penn said about James. It does not imply that James was incapable of violating the principles for which Penn stood or that Penn always knew exactly what was happening. It does not necessarily impugn the Glorious Revolution of 1688. Life, especially political life, goes beyond cold reason; and a monarch who antagonizes his nation, who calls into being, or exacerbates where they exist, even groundless fears, is almost ipso facto discredited. Even if James had been morally as

209

impeccable as Penn, he still would have been politically wrong in too many ways.

The theory simply vindicates Penn in the broad essentials of his position. It argues that he was basically right and his opponents wrong about three things: (1) the personality of James II; (2) the power balance between James and the kingdom; and (3) the alternatives to James. Restating the thesis, Penn was right in saying: (1) that James was sincere; (2) that James could not succeed if he were insincere; and (3) that James was a better choice to lead England than any of his adversaries.

(1). It is easier to believe Penn than to doubt him when he calls the King honest about wanting the widest freedom of opinion and the liberties consequent thereon. Penn was better equipped than anyone else to pass judgment on James Stuart; and no one ever has, in fact, refuted him. His word is, all things considered, the best we have. Even a modified Whig version of James II is more questionable than the knowledge, intelligence, and integrity of Penn. The critical fact, and one that cries aloud for explanation, is Penn's very fealty to James. The theory propounded here explains that fealty, and it is the only theory that does.

If it failed to take account of the other facets of James' reign, it still might be questioned; but this is not the case. Thus, Penn's contemporaries who disagreed with him about James' intentions, Bishop Burnet for example, can be proven wrong without forcing the evidence or special pleading. Puzzles about the reign still exist; but all we should look for, or have a right to expect, is a line of thought that covers most of the evidence, and more of the evidence than any other. This interpretation of Penn does just that.

(2). Much the same argument applies to James' capabilities, with this added strength, that Penn's judgment can be more easily supplemented from historical data. It is *beyond plausible reasoning that James could have destroyed English liberties and the Protestant denominations. Even if he had thrown William's invasion into the sea and returned to London flushed with victory, he still would have met opposition in Parliament, in London, in the counties, even in his armed forces. If he had been rash enough to drive forward regardless, he almost certainly would have raised up a nationwide insurrection that would have cost him his throne. If he had not been that rash, England might have subsided into the kind of political equilibrium envisioned by Penn. In short, James' capabilities were very nearly as Penn described them—enough to sustain religious toleration, not enough to Romanize the population.*

(3).   As for the alternatives to James, there was the possibility of continued persecution—which was becoming more and more indefensible at the time and probably would not be the preference of anyone now. The other alternative was the one that really frightened Penn, namely Whig and Anglican domination of the national life. He saw the realization of this with the Revolution Settlement. The Toleration Act outlawed the equality of denominations for which he had labored. Anglican superiority being now codified and systematized, England embarked on a long and dusty advance toward the type of indulgence Penn wanted and that he thought could be achieved under James II. His fellow countrymen would not catch up with him until the nineteenth century.

The whole argument points to the conclusion that James and Penn had a true understanding on one pivotal principle—the principle of religious toleration, equality for all the major faiths. They were agreed, that is, on the short-term objective of practical politics. James' long-range objective—the reconversion of England to Catholicism—was something Penn could shrug off as a mirage. He hoped that one day

England would go Quaker. James hoped it would go Catholic. These hopes were incompatible; but both were consistent with a mutual determination to take a step forward, here and now, into the preliminary stage of universal sufferance. It is unreasonable to doubt that James and Penn were aware of the historical dialectic that made them allies.

If this solution is sound, and on the basis of the evidence it seems ineluctable, it makes sense of more than the Penn–James connection. It makes sense of each man individually.

The twentieth century can only find extraordinary the spectacle of a ruler driven from his throne and then virulently denounced in the history books because he tried to give his subjects a sanction to worship as they saw fit without paying for it. This undeniable virtue in James need no longer be transmuted, somehow, into a vice. If we see him as a well-meaning fool—well-meaning because of his intentions, a fool because of the measures and the men he chose to realize them—then the facts about him slip into place without jostling one another. His broad-mindedness can subsist along with his injuries to the Church of England, his desire for Parliamentary support along with his attacks on the rights of Parliament, his English patriotism along with his French subsidies.

There is no compulsion to go to the other extreme and to pronounce his fall an unmitigated misfortune. England lost religious equality, but only temporarily. Had he not fallen on the other hand, Cabinet government would probably never have developed. Some co-partnership of King and Parliament might have been worked out, but there is no telling how long it would have lasted after James, or what it would have led to over the decades; and to prefer some hypothetical system to the English institutions now operating would be absurd. It is not proper to allege this against James (or Penn) in his own time. It is proper to do so by virtue of almost three

*centuries of experience since 1688. One can, with 20–20 hind-
sight, applaud the expulsion of James II without being pushed
to maintain that Penn ought not to have hindered the good
work.*

*The theory also makes sense of William Penn. No longer
need his biographers slide shamefacedly past the part of his
life that he himself probably considered the most important
of all. To have been instrumental in winning freedom of
conscience for his native land would have been for him a
momentous achievement, dwarfing his achievement in Pennsylvania. His efforts ought not to be minimized because of a
preconception that, the King being James II, something must
have been wrong. Give Penn's place at Whitehall the meaning
he gave it, and his career as an advocate of toleration becomes
monolithic, all of a piece—in England as in Pennsylvania and
on the Continent. Cavil because the King he served was
James II, and his career falls apart, leaving him the caricature
of a man who is really two men—one a majestic and perspicacious libertarian to whom all subsequent generations in
the West are beholden, the other a befuddled moron who
cannot recognize blatant hypocrisy when it is thrown in his
face. The available interpretations do not seem equally con-
vincing.*

*Looked at in the light of all this, the friendship between
the Catholic monarch and his Quaker subject becomes neither
inexplicable nor even extraordinary. No apology is called for.
There is more to be said for William Penn's loyalty to James
II than his admirers have been willing to concede.*

NOTES

THE PROBLEM

14   "the part that Penn took . . ." William I. Hull, *William Penn: A Topical Biography* (Oxford University Press, 1937), 264.

14   " possibly the unscrupulous and bigoted James . . ." Frederick B. Tolles and E. Gordon Alderfer, *The Witness of William Penn* (New York, 1957), xvii.

14   "the integrity of Penn . . ." Thomas Babington Macaulay, *The History of England from the Accession of James II,* Everyman ed. (London, 1906), I, 389.

15   "Penn actually had the face . . ." Sydney George Fisher, *The True William Penn* (Philadelphia, 1900), 284.

15   " It appeared to many . . ." Bonamy Dobrée, *William Penn, Quaker and Pioneer* (London, 1932), 210.

15   " No doubt the intentions . . ." C. E. Vulliamy, *William Penn* (New York, 1934), 209–10.

15   "An ardent believer in toleration . . ." David Ogg, *England in the Reigns of James II and William III* (Oxford University Press, 1955), 180.

16   "extraordinary, indeed inexplicable . . ." F. C. Turner, *James II* (London, 1948), 309.

THE BACKGROUND

1. Admiral Sir William Penn

19   "not equalled in his time . . ." John Aubrey, *Brief Lives,* ed. Anthony Powell (London, 1949), 362.

19   "constancy . . ." William Penn, *Truth Rescued from Imposture,* in *A Collection of the Works of William Penn,* ed. Joseph Besse (London, 1726), I, 496–97. Besse's edition is hereafter referred to as *Works.*

20   "could never be persuaded . . ." The Earl of Clarendon, *The History of the Rebellion and Civil Wars in England* (Oxford University Press, 1888), VI, 10.

20   " 'twas not so much . . ." William Penn, *Truth Rescued from Imposture,* 498.

21   "for a special service . . ." Granville Penn, *Memorials of the Professional Life and Times of Sir William Penn* (London, 1833), II, 221.

23   "you well know . . ." Ibid., 234.

23   "The duke," says Clarendon . . ." Ibid., 292.

2. The Penns: Father and Son

26   "extremely tender . . ." Aubrey, 360.

28   "Gross Ignorance . . ." William Penn, *Truth Exalted, Works,* I, 243.

28   " Hellish Darkness and Debauchery . . ." *Travails in Holland and Germany, Works,* I, 478.

30   "persecuted . . ." Ibid.

30   " Bred his sonne religiously . . ." Aubrey, 362.

31   "sober and religious People . . ." Joseph Besse, *The Author's Life, Works*, I, 2.

31   "the bitter usage . . ." *Travails in Holland and Germany*, 478.

33   "I was once myself . . ." William Penn, *No Cross, No Crown* (Philadelphia, 1872), 106.

34   "At my arrival at Harwich . . ." Samuel M. Janney, *The Life of William Penn: with Selections from His Correspondence and Autobiography*, 4th ed., (Philadelphia, 1876), 26–27.

35   "Remembering that formerly . . ." Ibid., 29.

35   "I wish your youthful desires . . ." Ibid.

36   "The Dutchmen's being in the river . . ." Granville Penn, II, 441.

36   "embezzling goods . . ." *Calendar of State Papers, 1667–1668* (London, 1893), 351.

38   "I vow, Mr. Penn . . ." Janney, 90.

39   "[William's] father . . ." Thomas Harvey, *The Convincement of William Penn*, in *The Journal of the Friends' Historical Society*, XXXII (1935), 24.

39   "In the morning . . ." Ibid.

40   "to make a difference . . ." *The History of the Life of Thomas Ellwood, Written by Himself* (London, 1675), 26.

40   "And here my Pen is diffident . . ." Besse, I, 4.

41   "Returning home . . ." Harvey, 25.

43   "If you are ordained . . ." Granville Penn, II, 572.

44   "But, which is most remarkable . . ." Aubrey, 362.

44   "she fell upon the strange rude way . . ." *The Penn-sylvania Magazine of History and Biography*, LXX (October, 1946), 361

44   "she said your father . . ." Ibid., 361–62.

45   "the most gracious and kind . . ." Granville Penn, II, 562.

45   "Son William, I am weary . . ." *No Cross, No Crown*, 408.

THE ESSENTIAL FACTS

3. William Penn, Charles II and the Duke of York

49   "When he had done . . ." William Penn, *Fragments of an Apology for Himself*, in *Memoirs of the Historical Society of Pennsylvania*, III (1834), 242.

52   "dark suggestions of Papal Superstition . . ." *A Seasonable Caveat against Popery*, in *Works*, I, 467.

52   "the Tribe of Men . . ." Ibid., 468.

52   "Their pretense . . ." Ibid., 470.

52   "they declared him an idolator . . ." *James Earl of Abingdon's Discourse with King James the Second, Nov. 18th, 1687, from his own Memorandum of it*, in *Supplementary Report on the Manuscripts of Montagu Bertie Twelfth Earl of Lindsey*, Historical Manuscripts Commission 79 (London, 1942), 271.

53   "The charges against Plunket . . ." G. N. Clark, *The Later Stuarts: 1660–1714* (Oxford University Press, 1940), 91.

54   "pursue the Discovery . . ." *England's Great Interest in the Choice of This New Parliament, Works*, II, 678.

54   "from Popery and Slavery . . ." Ibid.

54   "chuse Sincere Protestants . . ." Ibid., 681.

55   "I do not believe . . ." *One Project for the Good of England, Works,* II, 689.

56   "We may see here . . ." *England's Present Interest* (London, 1675), 28.

57   "I would not be mistaken . . ." *Works,* I, 118–19.

58   "By no Means chuse . . ." *England's Great Interest,* 680.

59   "Sidney's reputation . . ." *Dictionary of National Biography.*

59   "Thou, as thy friends . . ." Janney, 154.

60   "Shaftesbury had been . . ." J. H. M. Salmon, "Algernon Sidney and the Rye House Plot," in *History Today* (October, 1954), 700.

60   "Algernon Sidney is to be beheaded . . ." Sir John Dalrymple, *Memoirs of Great Britain and Ireland* (London, 1790), II, 115.

61   "I, A.B., do solemnly . . ." *One Project for the Good of England,* 689.

63   "To exact such an interminated tax . . ." Sydney G. Fisher, *The Quaker Colonies* (Yale University Press, 1919), 134–35.

64   "found things in generall . . ." *Fragments of an Apology* 235–36.

65   "I cast about in Mind . . ." Ibid., 236.

66   "Upon the whole Matter . . ." Ibid.

66   "And the Duke was as good as his word . . ." Ibid., 237.

4. The Court of James II

69   "the fearful Tale of Predestination . . ." *The Christian Quaker* (London, 1674), Preface.

69   "you generally scoff . . ." *Truth Exalted,* 244.

69   "that he looked upon us . . ." *Fragments of an Apology,* 242.

70   "We believe government to be . . ." *Works,* I, 118.

70   "the Unreasonable and Unmerciful Doctrine . . ." *England's Present Interest,* 55.

70   "O what did not . . ." *The Christian Quaker,* Preface.

71   "I can never think . . ." Ibid.

71   "The Independents themselves . . ." *A Persuasive to Moderation,* reprint in Occasional Papers of the California State Library (San Francisco, 1940), 249.
     "the English Phocas . . ." *An Apology for the Principles and Practices of the People Called Quakers, Works,* II, 86.

72   "a True Liberty of Conscience . . ." *Fragments of an Apology,* 238.

73   "the English Empire . . ." *Inedited Letters of William Penn,* in *Memoirs of the Historical Society of Pennsylvania,* III (1834), 291–92.

75   "For the love of God and me . . ." Robert Proud, *History of Pennsylvania* (Philadelphia, 1798), II, 297.

76   "He spoke very agreeably . . ." *The Works of Jonathan Swift,* ed. Sir Walter Scott (London, 1883), XII, 207.

76   "for whom exhibitions . . ." Macaulay, I, 507.

76 "seemed to take pleasure . . ." Ibid., 212.

78 "And the King often . . ." Gerard Croese, *Historia Quakeriana* (Amsterdam, 1695), 369.

79 "is very much in the King's confidence . . ." Turner, 287.

79 "urged the king forward so rashly . . ." Clark, 118.

79 "James had at his side . . ." George Macaulay Trevelyan, *England Under the Stuarts*, 19th ed., (London, 1947), 362.

80 "In his alarm Sunderland . . ." J. P. Kenyon, *Robert Spencer, Earl of Sunderland, 1641–1702* (London, 1958), 140.

81 "At this time the word . . ." Leopold von Ranke, *History of England Principally in the Seventeenth Century* (London, 1875), IV, 309.

82 "It is certain . . ." *Some Fruits of Solitude,* various editions, no. 352.

5. Penn as Censor of the Reign

84 "informed of for meeting . . ." *Fragments of an Apology,* 236.

84 "I mentioned thy friend Aaron Smith . . ." Charlwood Lawton, *A Memoir of Part of the Life of William Penn,* in *Memoirs of the Historical Society of Pennsylvania,* III (1834), 221.

86 "He said to me . . ." *Bishop Burnet's History of His Own Time* (Oxford, 1833), III, 66.

86 "About three hundred hanged . . ." Janney, 268.

87 "The maids of honour . . ." Macaulay, I, 500.

88   "unwarrantable assumption . . ." W. E. Forster, *William Penn and Thomas B. Macaulay*, 2nd ed. (Philadelphia, 1850), 10.

88   "This seemed demonstration . . ." J. R. Bloxam, *Magdalen College and James II: 1686–1688* (Oxford, 1886), 182.

89   "The courtly Quaker . . ." Macaulay, I, 731.

89   "An examination of the evidence . . ." Sir Charles Firth, *A Commentary on Macaulay's History of England* (London, 1938), 270–71.

      "Mr. Macaulay's perversions . . ." Forster, 24.

90   "With this object in view . . ." J. R. Tanner, *English Constitutional Conflicts of the Seventeenth Century* (Cambridge, 1928), 258.

91   "seems to me to be Unpacking . . ." *The Great and Popular Objection against the Repeal of the Penal Laws and Tests* (London, 1688), 14.

92   "that and several other anonymous letters . . ." Lawton. 224, 226.

92   "liked me for my sincerity . . ." Ibid., 225.

92   "desired his Majesty to consider . . ." Abingdon, 272.

94   "But before I go further . . ." Lawton, 230–31.

6. Penn, James, and Catholicism

99   "The Popish lords and gentry . . ." Hull, 242.

99   "He declared he concealed himself . . ." Janney, 264.

101   "Pardon me, we have not to do . . ." *A Persuasive to Moderation*, 223.

101   "owned that there were officers . . ." Clark, 116.

101   "I do very well remember . . ." *A Persuasive to Moderation*, 243.

102   "the two things men value most . . ." *English Historical Documents*, ed. Andrew Browning (London, 1953), 395.

102   "By this Grace . . ." *Works*, I, 130.

103   "Gentlemen, I thank you . . ." Ibid., 131.

105   "It is the first Lesson . . ." *The Great Case of Liberty of Conscience* (London, 1670), 23.

105   "the great Charters . . ." *A Letter to the Council and Senate of Embden, Works*, I, 611.

106   "For under favour . . ." Janney, 160.

108   "First, by Liberty of Conscience . . ." *The Great Case of Liberty of Conscience,* 11–12.

109   "If we are contributaries . . ." *First Frame of Government*, Pennsylvania Archives (Harrisburg, 1900), 25

109   "To Conclude, there ought to be . . ." *A Persuasive to Moderation,* 243.

110   "I did maintain it . . ." *A Reply to a Nameless Author, Works*, II, 810.

111   "Be pleased to consider . . ." *An Address to Protestants of All Persuasions*, 30.

114   "the timely Indulgence . . ." *The Great Case of Liberty of Conscience*, 41.

114   "It was a Huguenot . . ." *A Persuasive to Moderation,* 240.

115   "I know it is said . . ." *Good Advice*, 11.

115   "But let us see the end . . ." *A Persuasive to Moderation*, 235.

116   "Violence and Tyranny . . ." *Good Advice*, 42–43.

116   "Our Superiours governing themselves . . ." *England's Present Interest*, 38.

117   "Then it was . . ." *A Persuasive to Moderation*, 253.

117   "I know the principles of the Church of England . . ." Turner, 240.

120   "repeated the king's promise . . ." Clark, 120.

120   "To object the King's promise . . ." *Good Advice*, 15.

120   "And if the Church of England . . ." Ibid., 49–50.

121   "Be not Couzen'd . . ." Ibid., 55.

121   "I should not wonder . . ." The Earl of Halifax, *Letter to a Dissenter* (London, 1687), 4.

121   "their Master-piece . . ." *The Great and Popular Objection against the Repeal of the Penal Laws and Tests* (London, 1688), 8.

122   "The first is, the cause you have . . ." *Letter to a Dissenter*, 2.

122   "Consider that notwithstanding . . ." Ibid.

122   "It is a misfortune . . ." *Great and Popular Objection*, 15.

122   "That which moves him to it . . ." Ibid., 12.

122   "This Alliance . . ." *Letter to a Dissenter*, 3.

123   "So that tho it is true . . ." *Great and Popular Objection*, 20.

123   "they allow no living . . ." *Letter to a Dissenter,* 6.

123   "We look on France . . ." *Great and Popular Objection,* 9.

124   "If you had now to do with . . ." *Letter to a Dissenter,* 10.

124   "If she affects an Union . . ." *Great and Popular Objection,* 19.

124   "If she will please . . ." Ibid., 18–19.

125   "Are you so linked . . ." *Letter to a Dissenter,* 14.

125   "But that we should be less safe . . ." *Great and Popular Objection,* 6.

125   "cogent . . ." Sir Winston Churchill, *A History of the English-Speaking Peoples,* vol. II, *The New World* (London, 1956), 315.

126   "wholehearted enthusiasm . . ." Turner, 311.

126   "he abhorred the employment . . ." Ibid.

126   "His Majesty's royal goodness . . ." *The Prose Works of the Right Reverend Thomas Ken,* ed. William Benham (London, n.d.), 290.

126   "told his Majesty he would find . . ." Abingdon, 272.

127   "Whatever Practices . . ." *Works,* I, 135–36.

128   "We cannot but heartily wish . . ." *English Historical Documents,* 395–96.

129   "Your former faults . . ." *Letter to a Dissenter,* 14.

129   "And tho it is Imagined . . ." *Great and Popular Objection,* 16.

130   "Let us be still . . ." *Letter to a Dissenter,* 16–17.

130 "In my opinion, 'tis Groundless . . ." *Great and Popular Objection*, 8.

131 "a nation fanatically . . ." Turner, 395.

131 "What they convert . . ." *Good Advice*, 48–49.

132 "I say then this Unity . . ." Ibid., 48.

132 "the Intestine Division . . ." Ibid., 51.

133 "the handfull of half-unwilling. . ." Trevelyan, *The English Revolution, 1688–1689* (New York, 1939), 75.

133 "the Law is so sacred . . ." *Letter to a Dissenter*, 8.

134 "If we can but once see . . ." *Great and Popular Objection*, 22.

7. Penn, James, and English Liberties

139 "By Government we understand . . ." *The Great Case of Liberty of Conscience*, 23.

140 "When the great and wise God . . ." *First Frame of Government*, 24.

141 "that sovereign and independent state . . ." *An Essay towards the Present and Future Peace of Europe* (Philadelphia, 1944), 25.

141 "a reasonable design . . ." Ibid., 10.

142 "Government is an expedient . . ." Ibid., 8.

142 "is as hard to trace . . ." Ibid.

143 "Hence it is evident that . . ." *The Basic Works of Aristotle,* ed. Richard McKeon, (New York, 1941), 1129.

143 "This settles . . ." *First Frame of Government*, 25.

144   "there are three kinds . . ." Moses Amyraut, *Discours de la souveraineté des rois* (Saumur, 1650), 96.

144   "Government has many shapes . . ." *Fruits of Solitude*, no. 62.

144   "If any should ask me . . ." *An Address to Protestants of All Persuasions*, 196.

145   "are the Evil-doers . . ." Ibid., 197.

145   "Laws fundamental . . ." *The Great Case of Liberty of Conscience*, 48.

145   "Right Reason . . ." *An Apology for the Principles and Practices of the People Called Quakers*, 196.

146   "Let us use Methods . . ." *An Address to Protestants of All Persuasions*, 46.

148   "Let us compare . . ." Ibid., 232.

        "seems to be an Alteration . . ." *The Continued Cry of the Oppressed for Justice* (London, 1675), 4.

        "I know it is usually objected . . ." *England's Present Interest*, 28.

149   "Further let it be weighed . . ." *Works*, I, 169.

149   "The Parliaments of England . . ." *A Persuasive to Moderation*, 248.

150   "And in this we are . . ." *English Historical Documents*, 396.

150   "Certainly, if the Common Law . . ." *The People's Ancient and Just Liberties* (London, 1670, reprint 1908), 20.

150   "I appeal to the Jury . . ." Ibid., 23–24.

151   *"Mayor,* Sirrah . . ." Ibid., 16.

152   *"Recorder.* Sir . . ." Ibid., 21.

153   "The first and most fixt Part . . ." *The Continued Cry of the Oppressed for Justice,* 18.

153   "Where Liberty and Property . . ." *England's Present Interest,* 34.

153   "In England the Law is . . ." *The Excellent Privilege of Liberty and Property* (Philadelphia, 1897), 8.

154   "We are the People . . ." *To the Children of Light in this Generation* (London, 1678), 3.

154   "above all Kingdoms . . ." *England's Present Interest,* 6.

155   "I have been reported . . ." John Lingard, *The History of England* (London, 1883), X, 116–17.

156   "the technically illegal . . ." Clark 111.

157   "Grant that Parliament . . ." F. W. Maitland, *The Constitutional History of England* (Cambridge, 1908), 285.

158   "common sense was destined to triumph . . ." J. R. Tanner, *English Constitutional Conflicts of the Seventeenth Century* (Cambridge, 1928), 265.

159   "Apply yourself . . ." *Memoirs of the Chevalier St. George* (London, 1712), 41.

159   "He said it may be . . ." Abingdon, 271.

160   "Vassal! Vassal of France . . ." F. A. J. Mazure, *Histoire de la revolution de 1688 en Angleterre* (Paris, 1825), II, 165.

160   "represents James . . ." Dalrymple, 154.

164 "Pen said the king . . ." Burnet, III, 141.

166 "rightly regarding it . . ." Trevelyan, *England under the Stuarts,* 359.

166 "a military despot . . ." Ibid.

166 "a profound belief . . ." Ibid., 360.

166 "nine-tenths of (James') subjects . . ." Trevelyan, *The English Revolution,* 68.

166 "that God seem'd to raise . . ." *The Diary of John Evelyn,* ed. E. S. de Beer (Oxford, 1955), IV, 486.

166 "But certainly we must be . . ." *Good Advice,* 50.

168 "Let the people think . . ." *Fruits of Solitude,* no. 337.

8. The Glorious Revolution

170 "the inextinguishable Sunderland . . ." Clark, 213.

172 "Against the Earl of Clarendon . . ." *Report on the Manuscripts of the Late Allan George Finch,* Historical Manuscripts Commission, 71 (London, 1957), III, 128.

172 "I know false witnesses . . ." *Inedited Letters of William Penn,* in *Memoirs of the Historical Society of Pennsylvania,* IV (1840), 195.

172 "I do profess solemnly . . ." Ibid., 190.

172 "Let it be enough . . ." Ibid., 194.

172 "Mr. Penn is as much . . ." *Calendar of State Papers,* 20 January, 1691.

173 "The return which he made . . ." Macaulay, II, 790.

173 "I have been above these three years . . ." *Inedited Letters,* 198.

173 "But that an Englishman . . ." Ibid., 194.

174 "It would be too long . . ." *Calendar of State Papers,* 27 February, 1691.

174 "I will not receive . . ." *Inedited Letters,* 197.

180 "Whereas the late King James the Second . . ." *English Historical Documents,* 122.

181 "We do likewise declare . . ." Ibid., 396.

181 "Provided always . . ." *Documents Illustrative of English Church History,* ed. Gee and Hardy (London, 1896), 663.

183 "they humbly hope . . ." Thomas Clarkson, *Memoirs of the Private and Public Life of William Penn* (Philadelphia, 1814), II, 117.

184 "Seeing the Holy Scripture . . ." *Works,* II, 883.

186 "I beg this man's disgrace . . ." John Robert Moore, *Daniel Defoe, Citizen of the Modern World* (Chicago, 1958), 136.

9. Penn's "Naivete"

189 "Grace and Goodness . . ." *A Persuasive to Moderation,* 245.

189 "Humility, Plainness and Courage . . ." Ibid.

189 "Integrity . . ." Ibid., 224.

190 "Sir John Dalrymple . . ." Clark, 85.

191 "Art thou the last Witness . . ." *The New Witnesses Proved Old Heretics* (London, 1672), 38.

193   "magnified the King's Indulgence . . ." *The Petty—
       Southwell Correspondence* (London, 1928), 280.

193   "I acknowledge I was . . ." *The Friend,* VI (1833), 258.

194   "extreme satisfaction . . ." William Penn, *Fragments of
       an Apology,* 242.

194   "never found reason to doubt . . ." William Braithwaite,
       The Second Period of Quakerism (London, 1919), 118.

194   "In a word, if it had not been . . ." Burnet, IV, 540.

196   "The Revolution was the work . . ." Sir Charles Petrie,
       The Jacobite Movement: The First Phase (London,
       1948), 66.

198   "I might here add . . ." Anon., *Some Reflections upon
       Occasion of the Public Discourse about Liberty of Con-
       science* (London, 1687), 16.

198   "You will say perhaps . . ." William Darrell, *The Lay-
       man's Opinion, Sent in a Private Letter to a Considerable
       Divine of the Church of England* (London, 1687), 4.

198   "Whereas if the Toleration is Generall . . ." Richard
       Burthogge, *Prudential Reasons for Repealing the Penal
       Laws* (London, 1687), 9.

198   "There may be Laws made . . ." Giles Shute, *A New
       Test in Lieu of the Old One* (London, 1688), 4.

10. Penn, James, and the Historians

202   "James had already begun . . ." Hull, 257.

202   "greatest historic figure . . ." Lord Acton, *Lectures on
       Modern History* (London, 1906), 223.

202 "It was no secret . . ." Ibid., 219.

203 "it was only when the breach . . ." Trevelyan, *England under the Stuarts*, 356.

203 "Largely at Penn's instigation . . ." Ibid., 362.

203 "inexplicable . . ." See p. 16 above.

205 "No two men could have been . . ." Vulliamy, 210.

205 "anticipated modern liberalism . . ." Sir John Seeley, *The Growth of British Policy* (London, 1896) II, 254.

205 "He had a respect for law . . ." J. P. Kenyon, *The Stuarts* (New York, 1959), 160–61.

206 "The solution would be easier . . ." Lucile Pinkham, *William III and the Respectable Revolution* (Cambridge, Mass., 1954), 13.

206 "Perhaps one of the best pieces of evidence . . ." Ibid.

207 "due to his virtues as well . . ." Clark, 111.

207 "There is no real reason to doubt . . ." Ibid., 125.

207 "Let it be frankly admitted . . ." Petrie, 61–62.

207 "That the faults . . ." Ibid., 58.

BIBLIOGRAPHICAL NOTE

TO GIVE a comprehensive list of books would be superflous since so much of the text constitutes a critical biblography, and the pertinent sources may easily be discovered by consulting the notes. What follows here is simply a reminder of the few indispensable works that anyone should begin with if he wants to investigate the subject for himself.

No other piece of evidence has anything like the importance of William Penn's *Great and Popular Objection against the Repeal of the Penal Laws and Tests* (London, 1688). Penn wrote it professedly in defense of James II and as a reply to Halifax's *Letter to a Dissenter* (London, 1687), so that his position may here be observed in the round. There is no better approach to the problem than to read first Halifax and then Penn. Penn's two other key pamphlets should also be examined: *A Persuasive to Moderation* (London, 1686) and *Good Advice to the Church of England, Roman Catholick and Protestant Dissenter* (London, 1687). Much of his very revealing self-defense is in Samuel M. Janney, *Life of William Penn, with Selections from His Correspondence and Autobiography* (Philadelphia, 1852).

Once Penn's attitude is clear, the question of King James comes up. The King's own utterances and the official proclamations for which he was responsible may be found in standard works like *English Historical Documents* and the *Calendar of State Papers*. But since his honesty is the point at

233

issue and cannot be settled by an appeal to his words, it is
necessary to go to those modern scholars whose opinions of
James throw light on Penn's. Of these, three are eminently
to the purpose : G. N. Clark, *The Later Stuarts: 1660–1714*
(Oxford, 1940), Sir Charles Petrie, *The Jacobite Movement:
The First Phase* (London, 1948) and Lucile Pinkham, *William III and the Respectable Revolution* (Cambridge, Mass.,
1954). Herbert Butterfield's *The Whig Interpretation of
History* (London, 1950) is of the first importance as a critique
of the kind of thinking to which James II was almost always
subjected until comparatively recently.

INDEX